Selling in
a Skirt

SELLING IN A SKIRT

Selling in a Skirt

The Secrets Women Don't Know They Know About Sales (And What Men Should Know, Too)

JUDY HOBERMAN

SELLING IN A SKIRT

Selling in a Skirt

TABLE OF CONTENTS

SELLING IN A SKIRT

ACKNOWLEDGEMENTS

Whenever you start something from scratch, certain unknowns creep into your path. Sometimes they take you on a collision course and other times you simply find yourself navigating detours or speed bumps.

When I decided to start another phase in my life, everything was different. My life was different, the environment was different, the economy was different and most of all, I was different. Starting a new business was not a new concept for me, but I had to take all of those differences and see where they all fit and if they didn't fit I would have to change something. I did just that.

Those that know me know that control was something I thought I needed and wanted. I have discovered, in this phase of my life, that notion couldn't be any further from the truth. Although I still want to know how everything works and why it does, I have learned to delegate and take those tasks that I am not good at or don't really love and give them to someone on my team—and what a Dream Team I have.

Without the support of my children, Stephanie and PJ, I would be lost. They are the shining light that keeps me focused, and I have their shoulders to cry on and their excitement to celebrate with. They have always been my biggest fans and they still are. Having a son that is also your Web developer is an extra bonus.

Jason, my Social Media guru, has been a gift from above. Patience and innovation are his hallmarks. Coming back into the entrepreneurial arena at this advanced age, and having to learn all the newest approaches to marketing, is no easy task to teach. I was not even able to ask the questions I needed to ask, until Jason broke everything down for me. When someone finds me on Twitter, I am so excited, and when I tell him, he never says, "I told you so."

I am in awe of my red-headed twin and "editor" Gail for the way that the concept for my new venture kept materializing in front of her eyes. She has truly been an inspiration to me and the birth of *Selling in a Skirt*. I keep telling Gail I want to be her when I grow up, and I love being able to bounce ideas between us.

My "voice," Leslie, likewise dazzled me with her ability to figure me out so quickly, even when she didn't really know me. After spending so much time together every week deciding what belonged in this book and what didn't, I am so happy to call her one of my "girlfriends." I know it was not always easy to follow my thinking, but she did…and she never rolled her eyes.

Finally, Doreen, my business coach, forced me to see what was right in front of me and held me accountable for my results. She was sent to me when I was in turmoil, didn't believe I needed a coach and needed her more than she even realized. She was the first member of my Dream Team and started the ball rolling.

So many people have come into my life as I was building and marketing this company and writing this book. They have been supporters, cheerleaders and true friends. They have crossed state lines, including Texas, Tennessee, North Carolina, California, Nevada, Florida and Connecticut. I am so appreciative of everyone and rather than leave anyone out, this is a blanket thank you with love attached to you and you and you.

Selling in a Skirt is the newest addition to my family, and I hope you find one or two "a-ha!" moments between the pages. I am always looking for new stories and situations that would enhance the concept. If you have a story to share, I'd love to hear it. Who knows? You might just end up in my next book.

With love and great admiration,

~Judy

SELLING IN A SKIRT

FOREWORD

In the beginning ... that's where all stories begin. Some end with happily ever after, some end with a cliff hanger. This story began almost three decades ago when women were not well represented in the traditional corporate environment. Most women didn't work outside their homes as that was and still is a full-time career. However, for those brave enough to venture out into the workforce, the positions were typically teachers, administrative assistants and, in some cases, executive assistants. Sales was not a profession that most women dove into. Some stuck their toes in and were met with an undertow that could easily drag them down.

If women were lucky enough to find a company that would hire them, they had to be even more fortunate to find one that would train them. Most training programs followed a masculine model; after all, they were designed by men for men. A woman had to try and make this training fit. Added to this problem was that there were even fewer female role models to help guide women through this new frontier.

Today, the landscape is very different. Women are playing a more significant role in sales. In fact, many industries are dominated by female sales professionals. For the first time ever, women now make up 50 percent of the workforce, and more and more women are entering those professions that involve selling. Add that to the fact that women are responsible for more than 85 percent of consumer purchasing and you have the ingredients for a new and stronger market.

Now is the time to have a training program that addresses these converging markets. *Selling in a Skirt* provides the missing pieces that women are looking for. It isn't just a training program; it's a way of life for the next generation of successful saleswomen. Judy doesn't just talk the talk, she walks the walk. Her experience spans 28 years of working in male-dominated industries, and working hand-in-hand with the successful men that were her mentors.

Women are in full power when they honor and hone those talents and skills that are unique to them. The more we try to act like men, the best we can be is an imposter! *Selling in a Skirt* speaks to the distinctions between men and women. This program masterfully identifies the talents and strategies that women can apply and excel at when applied. Men will value this program, too, as it will help them in recruiting, training, motivating and retaining women on their team. Understanding and honoring these differences is important to both genders.

I highly recommend this book and the work that Judy Hoberman has developed here. She is a powerful woman who knows who she is and applies well-crafted and refined skills that every woman and man can embrace. *Selling in a Skirt* is a unique yet practical approach that can transform your results and create skyrocketing success.

Sandra Yancey
Founder & CEO
eWomenNetwork, Inc.
MyGLOW.net – a heart-centered social community for women who value authentic and uplifting interaction

SELLING IN A SKIRT

INTRODUCTION

When I first began my career in sales nearly 30 years ago, I was an anomaly. Outside of the retail environment, very few women worked in sales. In fact, women were still defining their role in the modern workforce, branching out from traditionally female careers, such as teaching and nursing, into previously male-dominated industries, like banking, insurance and medicine. Whereas women burned their bras to liberate themselves in the 1970s, they donned power suits-and-sneakers in the 1980s and took corporate America by storm.

Today, the number of women working in male-dominated businesses is at an all-time high, but their growing presence continues to create a variety of challenges for both genders. The conventional communication styles of men and women often are the source of misunderstandings, frustration, and even conflict in the workplace. In few fields is this issue more apparent than in sales. The traditional sales approach focuses on overcoming objections to achieve a quick close, but modern cultural trends point to a new paradigm: big numbers happen when sales people use "softer" collaborative and relational selling techniques.

Although many women have tried to incorporate this strategy into their own customer communications, they are often told by trainers and managers to avoid "experimentation" and to stick with time-honored tactics, however ineffectual. Several things happen as a result: female sales professionals find themselves using techniques that feel counterintuitive, male sales professionals may be missing opportunities to connect with women buyers, and male sales managers may fail to develop the innate talent of their female sales force.

My goal in writing this book is to shed light on the different ways that men and women think and communicate—both as buyers and as sellers—and invite readers to consider a new approach to sales. Far from being a book targeted only to women, *Selling in a Skirt* presents effective strategies for both sexes. The methodology outlined in this book is being implemented by forward-thinking sales managers who are garnering excellent results. They recognize that it's a buyer's market. Ultra-aggressive transactional sales can fail to deliver, and can also damage customer relations to the point of disrepair.

It's time to change the sales landscape—time to help both men and women understand how and why sales happen and the differences in selling to different populations.

Selling in a Skirt can be thought of as a road map that guides a new generation of salespeople through the sales landscape to reach their full potential. The ideas and strategies presented here can be used by both men and women to drive sales, increase referrals, and establish productive, long-term relationships with clients. As a modern guide to sales, *Selling in a Skirt* is also an informative learning experience for "traditional" (read: old school) salesmen and managers in understanding how to be effective communicators before, during, and after the sale.

This no-nonsense guide addresses gender-based talents and provides women and men with tips and tools they can use to take action immediately. The book will leave saleswomen and female managers feeling they can raise the bar and break any glass ceiling they previously perceived, using practical tools and methods for selling. For salesmen and male managers, it will uncover critical strategies that will help them to recruit, train, motivate and retain their female sales team.

Men and women really do think differently—and that's okay. By acknowledging and embracing these differences, we can improve communication with our co-workers and our customers. The following pages are filled with some of the most used and sought-after principles, examples, and action items that you can put into practice immediately.

Part One
THEN AND NOW

SELLING IN A SKIRT

CHAPTER ONE

CULTURE WARS

In the good old days, when Ward and June Cleaver ruled the television airwaves, selling was a man's job. Women didn't work in sales. Many didn't work at all—they were too busy shopping and keeping house.

Things began to change in the 1970s and 1980s, as women entered the workforce in droves. But gender stereotypes die hard, and although many women built successful careers as teachers, nurses and secretaries, the field of sales was still an "old boys' club." What's more, women's buying power remained primarily confined to personal items, like clothing, makeup and housewares. Women generally had little say in big-ticket purchases, such as insurance, home electronics and cars.

The last 20 years have marked a sea change, in terms of women's presence in the workplace and their economic influence as both wage earners and consumers. In fact, today women make or influence 85 percent of buying decisions. Sadly, however, many of the outdated perceptions of women's roles linger, particularly in the sales industry.

Traditional Training Tactics

Much of today's modern sales training still hearkens back to the work of thought leaders from the 1930s – 1990s, including:

- Dale Carnegie

- Tom Hopkins

- Elmer Wheeler

- Zig Ziglar

- Stephen Covey

- David H. Sandler (Sandler Selling System®)

These great communicators developed very detailed sales techniques, many of which are still viable and even highly effective in the modern marketplace. All of them, however, came from a predominantly male-centric viewpoint because, up until about 20 years ago, men sold to men.

For most of the 20th century, sales training focused on the art of persuasion. The salesman's efforts were aimed at convincing the other person to make a buying decision, whether through fear, intimidation, comparisons, philosophical questioning, or clever pricing strategies (e.g., "reducing it to the ridiculous"). In the end, the salesman was the victor and the buyer the vanquished.

The 1992 movie *Glengarry Glen Ross* is perhaps one of the best cinematic illustrations of the male-dominated, alpha-dog approach to sales. The story unfolds in a dingy, big-city real estate office, where the atmosphere is both despairing and cutthroat, and the communication among members of the all-male sales team is rife with profanity. Company representative Blake, brilliantly portrayed by Alec Baldwin, is downright abusive toward the salesmen as he throws down the gauntlet in the film's opening monologue:

> We're adding a little something to this month's sales contest. As you all know, first prize is a Cadillac Eldorado. Anybody want to see second prize? [*Holds up prize*]
>
> Second prize is a set of steak knives. Third prize is you're fired.
>
> A, B, C. A – Always. B – be. C – closing. *Always be closing.* Always be closing.
>
> A, I, D, A. Attention, Interest, Decision, Action. Attention – Do I have your attention? Interest – Are you interested? I know you are because it's f*** or walk. You close or you hit the bricks. Decision – Have you made your decision for Christ? And action – A, I, D, A.
>
> Get out there. You've got the prospects coming in. You think they came in to get out of the rain? A guy doesn't walk on the lot lest he wants to buy. They're sitting out there wanting to give you their money. Are you going to take it? Are you man enough to take it?

The film, based on a Pulitzer Prize-winning play by David Mamet, is a dark drama—yet, Blake's aggressive, take-no-prisoners approach hits close to home for those familiar with the old school sales mentality. There is no room for relationships in his sales strategy; it is all about completing the transaction. He sees the customer not as a person with interests and needs, but as a means to an end—another tick on the sales board, marking the progress toward a material prize.

SKIRT TIP Little more than a generation ago, the common practice of transactional sales focused on who would "win" the negotiation and set the customer up to be conquered rather than served. Today's consumers are savvier, and a relational approach to sales is more effective, particular with female buyers.

Discovering Mars and Venus

Fortunately, attitudes about sales and customer service have changed significantly in the past two decades. Many experienced trainers teach a more consultative approach to sales designed to engage customers in a dialogue and empower them to make a decision they feel confident about. Modern sales techniques focus on establishing trust, rather than trying to out-maneuver clients, in essence trapping them into making a purchase. As far as we have come, however, only a handful of businesses have acknowledged the importance of gender differences in the sales process as it relates to the most effective way of approaching the customer. The continued focus on completing a transaction rather than building a relationship means that companies are literally leaving money on the table, and leaving female customers feeling like second class citizens.

Moreover, women's natural gender-based talents generally go unrecognized and underused by sales trainers. Today, women have a much stronger presence in the sales industry—in fact, 11.7 percent of employed women worked in sales and related occupations in 2009, compared to 10.7 percent of men, according to the U.S. Department of Labor Bureau of Labor Statistics. Despite these statistics, women are still being trained by men on how to use sales techniques that work from a male perspective. These techniques not only fall flat with female consumers, but also frustrate female sales professionals. They often feel uncomfortable using male communication styles and defeated when the techniques fail to deliver positive results.

SKIRT TIP

Training a woman to sell like a man discounts her natural communication style, and the approach can be off-putting to female customers.

To be successful as a sales professional, you need to understand that men and women communicate differently. *Different does not mean that either communication style is better.* Men and women simply employ differing techniques to share and process information, based on innate as well as learned communication strategies. These differences shape how men and women form opinions and make decisions. Embracing these differences can facilitate the sales process and bolster customer retention, because a happy customer is a loyal customer.

When Worlds Collide

Research shows that men and women display specific behavioral characteristics for both verbal and non-verbal communication, some of which are based on acculturation and learning, and some of which are hard-wired into our brains. Although not all men or women will fit the stereotype, awareness of these gender differences can foster more productive interactions and build trust.

These different communication styles developed long before we started working. In childhood, girls are told to be ladylike and use their manners. Boys are encouraged to play roughly and loudly. Boys like things and how they work, girls are interested in people and relationships. Girls are allowed to show their feelings if they are hurt and are nurtured, while boys are told to be tough and not to cry. Girls play together and develop relationships while interacting. Boys play team sports and are competitive. (Again, if you are reading this and remember you played field hockey as a girl and were wildly competitive, keep in mind these character traits are from studies conducted regarding the differences in gender. There are always exceptions to the rule.)

Now fast forward through childhood to the workplace. Dr. Deborah Tannen uses the terms "Report

Talk" and "Rapport Talk" in her book *Talking from 9 to 5: Women and Men at Work*. Male communication traits tend to be honest, direct and factual—"report" talk. Women tend to be less direct, more tactful, and focus on connection—"rapport" talk. In essence, men tend to be more data-driven and communicate in bullet points; women are more experiential and use a narrative style. To have effective communication, understanding these differences is critical. Here are some facts regarding the differences in communication:

A WOMAN'S PERSPECTIVE	A MAN'S PERSPECTIVE
Women want to discuss problems	Men want to solve problems
Women feel comfortable expressing their feelings	Men view expressing their feelings as a sign of weakness
Women like recount stories	Men like to cut to the chase
Women like to talk about issues	Men like to get to the source of a problem
Women like sharing information to build relationships	Men enjoy giving information to demonstrate their expertise
Women listen to gain understanding of a speaker's experience	Men listen to solve problems
Women are better at sharing a dialogue	Men are better at delivering a monologue
Women connect	Men compartmentalize
Women value relationships and cooperation	Men value power and status
Women want to immerse you in their world	Men want to give you just the bullet points

Can You Hear Me Now?

As in almost every aspect of life, men and women also listen differently. Men listen to find out what the point is or what the problem is. They are focused on determining the most important part of the conversation and using this information to solve the problem. Any information in the middle is generally tuned out. Women will want to gather all the information and find out what is needed to give an appropriate solution—but a woman can't offer this solution unless there is a beginning, a middle and an end to the story. For women, the middle is key.

In fact, in a study conducted by the Indiana University School of Medicine, researchers monitored the brain activity of 20 men and 20 women while the subjects listened to an audiotape of a novel. The results indicated that the men listened only with their left brain, which controls *listening* and speech. The women had brain activity in both sides of the brain—the left side and the right side, which is associated with creativity and imagination. This research suggests that men and women process language differently.

Case in Point: Men and Women Listen Differently

Let me give you an example of how men and women listen differently. In one of my field training sessions, I had a brand new salesperson with me. We had been together in the field for a few weeks and on this particular day he asked whether he could do the presentation. I agreed because he had seen me do this enough times. I reminded him that he needed to ask questions to determine what the client's needs were and then simply sit back and listen.

We entered this beautiful home in an extremely affluent area. As we walked in I told him I would be his safety net and would not jump in unless it was necessary. He smiled and I could see how excited he was. When we sat down, the client let us know what his needs were before we even asked. We were presenting insurance and because he was wealthy, he was not concerned with the "little" things. His concern was to protect his assets. I knew what type of plan we needed to present but kept quiet so that the new salesperson would have the opportunity to put together his solution.

With everything but this client's 1099 in front of us, the new associate began discussing the co-pay for doctor's visits. It was clear that the client was not worried about co-pays—he was more interested in protecting his assets. My colleague was not listening to the client.

I ended up finishing the appointment and we were able to help address his needs. What could have been a losing situation ended up with a completed application—but only because I stopped the conversation and restated the needs of the client. I made sure he knew that I was not only hearing what he said, but was also listening and able to offer appropriate solutions.

Listening is the key to selling and is one of the most important aspects in the sales process. By simply asking the right question and then stopping to listen, you will get all the information you need to help solve a problem, address a concern and ultimately give your client what he or she is really looking for.

But make no mistake, there is a difference between hearing and listening. Hearing is the act of perceiving sound by the ear. Unless you are hearing-impaired, hearing simply happens. Listening, however, is something you consciously choose to do. Listening requires concentration so that your brain processes meaning from words and sentences. Listening leads to learning. In other words, hearing is when the sound reaches your ears. Listening is when it reaches your brain. Most people tend to be "hard of listening" rather than "hard of hearing." Unfortunately, it is human nature to speak more than we listen, even though we have two ears and one mouth. If you want to be successful, whether in your personal or professional life, you have to learn to listen first. You will have an opportunity to speak soon enough.

SKIRT TIP

You can demonstrate active listening by reframing the speaker's statement and asking for confirmation.

Strategies for the New Millennium

Recognizing the different communication styles of men and women can empower you to adjust your own communication style and sales approach to better meet the needs of your customer. Regardless of whether you are male or female, you can adapt your language and listening skills to address the desires and expectations of your client, increasing customer satisfaction and ultimately improving your bottom line. Since more than 8 out of 10 buying decisions are made or influenced by women, focusing on the way women communicate and shop can have a marked impact on your close ratio.

In the next several chapters, we will explore what women want when making a purchase and look at ways to hone your sales strategy for women buyers. If you are a female sales associate, you will also learn to nurture your inherent relational skills to build trust and win more business. If you are a male sales professional, you will learn how taking the time to talk with female buyers at length can help them feel heard, and foster a trusted relationship that can not only lead to a sale, but also result in frequent referrals. Finally, we will examine training strategies designed to empower and retain female sales professionals to the benefit of your organization.

SKIRT WISDOM

- Men and women communicate differently, which mandates a different sales approach.

- Men focus on exchanging information, whereas women focus on building relationships.

- Male-centric sales techniques usually fall flat with female customers, who want the process to be more personal.

- Embracing the different decision-making styles of men and women can make sales go much smoother.

- Listening is critical in sales, particularly when selling to women.

CHAPTER TWO

A NEW ERA

Our grandmothers and even our mothers may have had little say when it came to large, costly purchases for the home and family. Today, however, the female population carries tremendous financial clout. Consider these statistics:

- Women account for 85 percent of all consumer purchases, including everything from cars to computers to health care, and spend about $5 trillion annually—more than half the U.S. gross domestic product. – *She-conomy*

- 52 percent of corporate middle managers are women. – *"Sexism," Portfolio.com (2008)*

- 30 percent of working women out-earn their husbands. – *"I Am Woman, Hear Me Shop," BusinessWeek Online (2005)*

- Senior women age 50 and older control net worth of $19 trillion and own more than three-fourths of the nation's financial wealth. – *MassMutual Financial Group (2007)*

Clearly, women have serious buying power—so why are the majority of sales professionals still men, and why are they using predominantly male-centered sales techniques?

The Rules of Engagement

In a recent survey, 91 percent of women said that advertisers don't understand them. The same, I believe, could be said of sales associates. I have heard and read countless stories from women who have been slighted, disrespected or flat out ignored during the buying process. Despite their financial muscle, women are still perceived as lacking the influence or the intellect to make important buying decisions.

Much of the disconnect stems from the way that men and women engage in the buying process. In general, when men go to make a purchase, they have a clear idea of what they want and their intention is to make a swift sales transaction and be done with it. If they had any questions about their purchase, they likely did their due diligence in advance, researching online or getting input from friends and colleagues.

For women, on the other hand, shopping is experiential—it's a process, not a transaction. They tend to ask a lot of questions and take in all of the details of the environment (lighting, music, etc.). They size up the sales associate based on everything from his or her mode of dress to the salesperson's expression of sincere interest. They take into consideration not only their own needs, but anyone else who is going to be affected by the purchase.

For example, if a man goes to buy a suit for a special occasion, he will want to know that it's well-made, that it fits, and that it is within his budget. He doesn't care what the store looks like (as long as it's clean and he can find what he needs), and he doesn't want to engage in small talk with the salesperson. He wants a suit, and if he finds a suit, he's happy.

In contrast, if a woman goes to buy a little black dress for a special occasion, she will start to size up the buying experience from the minute she walks in the store. What is the mood? Are the lighting and music appealing? Is the salesperson welcoming and personable, or are they pushy/condescending/impatient? All of these factors will influence the woman's buying decision. Then, once she finds a dress she likes, she likely will ask herself a litany of questions, such as:

- Does it suit the occasion?
- Does it make me look fat?
- Does it make me look *thin*?
- Do I have accessories to go with it?
- Do I have shoes to go with it?
- Can I wear it again?
- Does it show too much cleavage?
- Does it look cheap/expensive?
- What are the odds that someone from this event will see me in the same dress at the next event?
- Can I afford it?
- If I can't afford it, will my husband kill me if I get it anyway?

In short, men buy, women shop.

SKIRT TIP Trying to circumvent a woman's thought process to push for a swift close can make buyers feel insecure and mistrusting. Learn to embrace the process and walk through it together to form a strong connection with female customers.

In her book *Make a Fortune Selling to Women,* Connie Podesta, an expert in the psychology of human behavior and acclaimed executive coach, explains that women want the shopping experience to be personal, professional and positive—they want to be treated with kindness and respect. Equally important, they want to be part of the process and for the overall experience to be productive. When a woman sets out to buy something, she has as much intention and desire to complete the purchase as a man does; however, the way she comes to that point will be very different. Women have an inherent desire for relationship, even when buying something as mundane as an air filter.

Notes Podesta, "Women develop feelings about every aspect of the process and those feelings drive their decision to buy from you—or not buy from you." Whereas men focus on the end result of the transaction, women assess the entire experience, focusing not just on features and price but on whether they like and trust the salesperson and feel the personal connection that will motivate them to buy. Understanding this dynamic is crucial to effective selling.

The $64,000 Question

External factors aside, much of the difference in how men and women approach buying decisions lies in the way they ask questions as part of the decision-making process. If a sales professional does not recognize or adapt to these differences when communicating with a female buyer, the sale can be easily lost.

Research indicates that women talk more than men. In fact, they talk a *lot* more than men. Women use about 20,000 words in a given day, compared to only 7,000 words for the average man, one study shows. Women also typically ask more questions than men, because questions are an effective means of establishing dialogue and help to keep a conversation flowing. This dialogue is fundamental to the buying experience for women.

Case in Point: The Importance of Questions

A few years ago, the lease on my car was near its end, and I began the search for a new vehicle. I had narrowed the decision down to two cars. I went to the first showroom and a salesman offered to help me. He asked whether I was ready to purchase a car that day. I definitely was, but he never asked me any further questions—not even what color car I wanted. When I told him I had some questions about the model I was considering, he rolled his eyes. He threw away the sale at that very moment. I forged ahead and asked him several questions, even making up a few, just to see what kind of customer service loomed ahead for me. From his responses—or lack thereof—I could tell he was obviously not interested in building a relationship, short- or long-term, with me.

I went to the next dealer with my guard already up. As the salesman approached me, the sales professional in me wanted to scream a warning to prepare him for what was coming. But he totally caught me off guard by politely saying, "Car shopping can be tortuous sometimes and I am hoping I can make this a pleasant experience for you. How and where can we begin?"

My entire attitude changed. I knew I had found a home: I was in a comfortable, pressure-free environment where I could ask questions. I told my salesman what happened to me at the first dealership and he laughed. He said he grew up with six sisters, and between them and his mom, he knew how women like to be treated and would do nothing less than treat women like family.

I not only purchased a car that day, but also referred two of my friends who bought cars that week. I have been a repeat client for that sales pro ever since. Don't you wish that kind of pleasant experience would happen in every part of your life?

The difference in the two car dealerships was the willingness of the salesmen to *ask* and to *answer* questions. The first salesman built a barrier when he rolled his eyes and showed his impatience with my questions (which meant he lost the sale!). The second salesman eliminated barriers by asking, essentially, "How can I help *you*?"

A woman's tendency to deliberate out loud and approach a purchase decision from multiple angles is part of her natural thought process. Most women are more experiential than transactional, and they are taking in a wealth of information as they calculate the pros and cons of their purchase. If a female buyer starts asking questions, rejoice! Seize the opportunity to engage in conversation and really connect. The more questions a woman asks—the more she thinks out loud and wants to discuss the product or service she is considering—the more vested she is in the buying process. You may spend more time with the customer, but you're also far more likely to win her business—and even garner referrals—in exchange for your effort.

The Great Debate

In addition to the tendency to ask questions during the sales process, women often take longer to make a purchase than men do. They want to think things over, whether for a few minutes or a few days. Often, salesmen will assume that a woman's propensity to ponder means she's indecisive. That is not the case; rather, women simply put more time and research into their decisions so that they can feel more confident about the purchase in the long run. Beverly Langford, author of *Closing the Gender Gap: Communication Styles of Women vs. Men,* notes that because women are more lateral thinkers, they often solve problems in a way that may seem illogical to their male counterparts.

Giving a female buyer the breathing room to "think things over" (while continuing to answer questions and maintain a positive attitude) ultimately can benefit you greatly. Once a woman feels confident in her decision to buy, she will be loyal to your business and happily refer you to her family and friends. When a woman has a good experience, she wants to share it.

Whether you're male or female, you need to understand how women think, communicate and buy. Remember, women influence 85 percent of all buying decisions! To be competitive in the modern economy, companies need a new paradigm—a new way of thinking about sales—that acknowledges and empowers women as both buyers and sellers. We'll explore some of those strategies in the next chapter.

SKIRT WISDOM

- Women view shopping as experiential, not transactional.

- Women want to feel a sense of connection; they want the salesperson to take a sincere interest in their needs.

- Women want their questions to be taken seriously and to feel important.

- A woman's tendency to deliberate does not mean she is indecisive.

- Adapting to a woman's communication style can result in a loyal customer and ongoing referrals.

SELLING IN A SKIRT

Part Two
DOING THINGS DIFFERENTLY

SELLING IN A SKIRT

CHAPTER THREE

RELATIONSHIP SELLING

Job seekers often recount the old adage, "It's not what you know, it's who you know." The same maxim applies to sales when dealing with female customers. Although knowing your product is important, for a woman, knowing and understanding *her* as an individual is even more so. Women want you to take the time to learn about their families, their careers and their lifestyles— even if only for a few minutes—so you can understand the larger context in which they are making a decision to buy from you. Information that may seem incidental or even irrelevant to a male sales professional can be a fundamental part of the equation for a female shopper.

In "Men Buy, Women Shop," a study by Wharton's Jay H. Baker Retail Initiative and the Verde Group, a Toronto consulting firm, researchers found that women value personal interaction with sales associates during the shopping experience more than men. Women think of shopping as inter-personal, according to the researchers, whereas men view it as a line item on their "to do" list.

Research indicates that female salespeople are better at establishing a long-term relationship with a customer, are better listeners, and find it easier to identify emotions and respond with empathy. Female salespeople start from a very different place than their male counterparts. Women start with the relationship rather than offering quick fix solutions that are typically a male trait. Women tend to be better listeners, and men are better at asking for the business. Women are more patient and men are more direct. Women like to build the relationship, and men like to "consummate" the relationship with the sale.

SKIRT TIP

Women's inherent tendency to engage in dialogue and build relationships is a powerful asset in a sales scenario.

When I started in sales, we had one product to sell and the chances of you seeing this particular client again were slim. I was told to work from the basis of "Slam, bam thank you ma'am"—but that was not a comfortable concept for me. I had asked why wouldn't I treat each client as a friend and make myself an all-around resource for them. The response was simply that my idea was ridiculous and would take too much time. But I forged ahead with building relationships. It wasn't long before the rest of my office was asking me how I received so many referrals.

For women sales professionals and for women

buyers, a successful transaction hinges on whether they establish a relationship with one another. So, how is this accomplished?

Winning a Woman's Trust

To start a relationship off on the right foot, you must first help the other person overcome any initial feelings of awkwardness. Whether striking up a conversation with a new contact at an industry conference or shaking hands for the first time with a prospective client, the eventual success of a relationship depends in large part on your ability to break the ice from the outset.

Why is breaking the ice so critical? It's the first step in building rapport. Rapport is important, because people buy from people they like. For men, however, the initial banter is kept to a minimum. Men prefer to dive straight into product talk, make a decision, and be done with their shopping. They don't want to shop—or talk—any longer than is absolutely necessary. For women, on the other hand, building rapport is more than a formality. Women want to connect. Your efforts to make a female client feel at ease demonstrate a desire for dialogue and create a foundation of trust. If a woman likes you but doesn't trust you, chances are slim that you will close the sale. If she likes you *and* trusts you, you may have a client for life.

To establish trust, you also need to bring real solutions. Friendly conversation isn't enough. Your goal is not to make the sale, but to help your customer. When you focus on bringing thoughtful solutions to meet her needs, trust is the natural outcome. To do this effectively, you must identify what those needs are.

Just the Facts, Ma'am

You cannot solve a problem without first identifying the real underlying issue. To solve a potential challenge for the customer, you must determine:

1) The client's current situation

2) Her ultimate needs and wants

3) The difference between the two

The most effective way to accomplish these goals is through *fact-finding*. Fact-finding is the process of asking questions to learn as much as you can about the other person. The more questions you ask, the more you will find out about your client. Likewise, the more questions you answer, the more your client will connect with you.

SKIRT TIP

Taking a vested interest in solving problems for the customer is highly effective when selling to women.

The true secret to fact-finding is to answer all the questions, no matter how trivial they may seem to you. Your job is to focus on your client's needs and connect with the client to find a solution together, asking questions that will encourage her to talk, such as:

- "What problems are you trying to solve?"

- "Tell me, what is important to you?"

- "What type of [product] do you have right now?"

- "What is your primary focus today?"

In short, you are engaged in *consultative selling* as opposed to *transactional selling.*

Case in Point: Fact-Finding to Discover Answers

I remember one occasion when I was on my way to an appointment and had a fairly new salesperson with me. We were working for an insurance carrier, and my colleague asked whether I had printed out the quote so he could review the details before we got to the appointment. I never print anything out and I never assume I know what the client needs...until I do some fact-finding. I had been in the business for four years and he had worked in sales for about four weeks. He had traveled with others that had printed out their quotes and naturally assumed I would do the same.

When we arrived at the appointment, the woman gave me a scenario that involved at least a dozen different situations that could happen and wanted to know whether and how she would be protected in each of these situations. I addressed every question and asked why these issues were important to her. She conveyed a story about a friend whose family struggled because they didn't have the appropriate insurance coverage. By the end of the appointment, she decided on coverage not only for herself, but for the rest of her family, as well. If I had printed a quote for just her, as my colleague had suggested, the sale would have turned out much differently. The key strategy in this situation was to avoid assumptions and ask questions to determine exactly what the client needed.

Three Steps to Success

Traditional sales strategies are generally linear in nature, with the sales associate driving the conversation and steering the prospect to a swift close. The focus is on the sales transaction, rather than on the relationship. This approach can be very off-putting to women, who may feel disrespected, misunderstood, or even bullied as a result. In contrast, *consultative selling* focuses on relationship-building, which is highly valued by women consumers. Remember, women make 85 percent of all buying decisions! Although the sales process can take longer, your success rate with female prospects will be exponentially higher when you invest the time and energy to establish a connection.

Effective *consultative selling* uses a combination of three techniques:

- "Open-ended" rather than "yes or no" questions

- Attentive listening

- Approval questions

Your initial fact-finding questions will be closed-ended questions. These are the questions that help you gather information or facts. They have set answers, such as "yes" or "no" or multiple choice answers, and don't leave a lot of room for conversation. In contrast, open-ended questions invite the prospect to describe in detail her needs and objectives. Your aim is to listen carefully to what she is saying, and also to what isn't being said. Attentive listening involves getting clarification, when necessary, so you can find the right solution—not just the one that best suits your own objectives. Once you determine that solution, you can transition to asking approval questions and get the green light to proceed toward the close.

SKIRT TIP

Consultative selling is all about engagement. You are fully present in the conversation, rather than rushing toward the finish line.

The process of discovering the facts should not simply be a series of questions and answers. After all, you don't want to make the client feel like they are being interrogated. Similarly, you should set aside any preconceived notions about what your prospect needs. Often, a sales associate will approach fact-finding with a firm idea about what they are going to sell, before finding out what the client really wants. Your goal should be to help the person determine those needs for themself and in doing so increase their motivation to buy from you.

Opening the Door

Open-ended questions help the prospect state their needs in their own words. Think of open-ended questions as "talk-show host" questioning. Imagine you had just sailed around the world, alone, in a sailboat in very difficult conditions. If you went on a talk show and the host asked you "Were you afraid?" your answer could be yes or no and that would be your entire answer. However, imagine if you were asked, "You were all by yourself, the conditions were horrific—what was your scariest (or most exciting) moment?" This kind of open-ended question would elicit a much different response.

Asking open-ended questions also encourages customers to talk about themselves and walk through "what if" scenarios in their minds that can help them feel more confident in their decision to buy.

Here are a few examples of open-ended questions:

- Why are you looking for [this product]?

- What are your biggest concerns?

- Which features are on your must-have list?

The aim with your initial questioning is to start a dialogue. Listening skills are vital. You may be tempted to jump into a sales pitch after the first two or three questions, but honestly, the client doesn't care about everything you have to say. Sure, they need to hear the features and benefits, and product knowledge is critical, but they love to talk about themselves. What better outlet than *you*?

If you ask the right questions, you will get more information than you will ever need to make a sale.

SKIRT TIP
To be a successful sales professional in today's customer-focused environment, you must like people. If you don't take a sincere interest in your customers' well-being, you are in the wrong line of business.

Listen and Learn

Of course, asking questions does little good if you don't make note of the answers. It is essential that you focus on your listening skills to have well-rounded communication. To a woman, good listening skills include making eye contact and reacting visually to whoever is speaking. To a man, listening can take place with a minimum of eye contact and almost no non-verbal feedback. Similarly, when a man nods, it means he agrees. When a woman nods, it means she is listening, but she may or may not agree with the statement. So learn to watch for non-verbal cues, like fidgeting or a furrowed brow, as well as verbal cues to understand where your client is at in the decision-making process.

Remember that people buy for their reasons, not yours. Restating what a prospect just said demonstrates that you are actively listening and summarizes your understanding of their situation, which in turn will highlight the prospect's motive for considering your products.

Similarly, asking follow-up (checking) questions can

help you determine whether your understanding of the situation is accurate. For example:

- "The reason you are considering [your product/service] is_____... Is that correct?"

- "Staying within your budget is your biggest concern today, is that right?"

- "Do I understand correctly that _____ is more important to you than _____?"

When in doubt, continue to ask fact-finding questions until you feel that you have a solid handle on the client's needs and desires. Do remember, however, that you may have to rein in the client if a response becomes a dissertation.

SKIRT TIP

Remember, your conversation has a purpose. You want to engage with the customer, but don't let the dialogue turn into coffee talk. Stay focused on your shared goal of finding a workable solution for the client's needs.

Getting to Yes

As the conversation continues, you will gradually transition from fact-finding and follow-up questions to approval questions. These are designed to help you get confirmation from the client, and to help the client know that you hear and understand her needs. Examples of approval questions include:

- "So, what you're saying to me is _____?"

- "What you're looking for is _____, do I understand that right?"

- "If we can do _____, that's what you're aiming for, yes?"

One final question that may not seem like an approval question is the ultimate catch-all, "Is there anything else?" Most men gulp and sweat at this, because they feel it is opening up Pandora's box. *What if she* does *have more questions? What if the appointment takes another hour? What if I don't have all the answers?* Worrying about the what-ifs will only present a road block to your goal of building a relationship. Once you get to that question, "Is there anything else?" you are really getting to the final buying decision. If the client does have additional questions, you can walk through them with confidence as you have been doing throughout the conversation. The client feels heard and that you cared enough to address all her concerns—a powerful experience for female buyers. If the client doesn't have any more questions, the close is a natural part of the process. In both cases, you are establishing the foundation of a long-term relationship.

Questioning takes time and patience. The technique often comes naturally to women and can seem onerous to men. In either case, however, if you nurture a collaborative communication style and build a relationship, *you may not close the first time out*, but the client will trust you and turn to you. Using this approach, you can have a longer, stronger relationship over time.

Grace Under Pressure

Asking questions to build a relationship cuts both ways. Not only will you be asking questions to your client in hopes of establishing trust and creating a connection, but your client might also have some questions for you. How you handle them can make or break the sale.

When considering a purchase, men generally ask questions for one purpose only: to gather information. For women, asking questions serves two purposes: to gather information and to cultivate the relationship. For women, it's all about connecting—connecting with the salesperson, their business, and others. As a salesperson, it is up to *you* what kind of connection will be made.

In her book *GenderTalk Works*, leading communications expert Connie Glaser notes that women ask three times as many questions as men do. They will ask ordinary inquiries, such as "Where did you leave the car keys?" as well as more leading questions, like, "Know what happened to me this morning…?" to kick off a conversation. Women are also more likely to tag the end of a sentence with a question, like, "We should have enough time for the connecting flight, don't you think?"

If you are a man, you may find a woman's tendency to ask questions unusual, if not flat out annoying. The fact remains, however, that most women cannot move forward until all their questions are answered. Men exchange information, whereas women have a *relationship* with the information they exchange. And because women have a relationship with information, they also have a relationship with everything they buy.

Case in Point: Women Want to Know

Early in my career, one of my first sales positions was with a burglar alarm company. During my training, I was told not to ask any questions about how the alarm worked because it was such a "simple" process—and I was assured that the clients wouldn't ask any questions, either. I was told, "Just demonstrate the product and it will sell itself. Don't ask them what they want or need. Have the 'package' put together and get in and out. You will be dealing with the husband and he wants to protect his family."

I was young and new to the job, so I followed my trainer's instructions. I arrived at the client's home, walked in, introduced myself and proceeded to set up the alarm. I was stopped dead in my tracks by the female client, who immediately started asking me question after question: "How does it work? Is it connected to the police? Why is this alarm different than others? How many customers does the alarm company have? Could you provide me with some referrals of happy customers?" I couldn't believe the number of questions she had, but I did my best to answer them—even though I hadn't been prepared for those questions during my training. Two hours later, the appointment ended and my clients said they needed to think about the product and would let me know their decision the next morning. When

I returned to the office, my manager told me that I must have done something wrong to prompt all those questions and to have not made the sale. The female client asked those questions because she wanted to establish rapport with me *and* with the product I was selling. I imagine my manager was not aware of the necessity of building relationships.

Closing the Deal: ~~Don't~~ Be Such a Girl

You've gone through the entire sales process and now you are ready to close the deal. If the preceding steps in the sales process have gone smoothly, closing the sale should be the next natural step. But getting here is not always the route you anticipated.

Ultimately, you have to ask for the business—and this is where many female sales associates fall short. After engaging in a dialogue with the client to get to know them and understand their needs, asking for the business can feel too calculated or disingenuous. Men, on the other hand, often ask for the business too soon, before the female customer is finished asking questions and reached a point of comfort that will result in a decision to buy.

A sound approach is to see the close as an integral part of the relationship. You get to the point of closing because you have addressed all of the client's needs and concerns and found a solution that they can feel good about. The only trick is to know when to pull the trigger.

SKIRT TIP When you understand a customer's needs and have addressed all their questions, you can feel good about closing the sale because you are offering a workable solution to their problem. You are operating from a foundation of trust and goodwill.

In some instances, you are reading the buying signals that let you know that this client is going to close. They are starting to think more, talk less and give you positive feedback. In other instances you think they are ready to close and they tell you they need to think about it when there is still an objection hanging out there. In yet another instance, they are ready to close, just not today. You can recognize these three distinct scenarios in the sales process:

Scenario #1: All Systems Go!

This is always the preferred situation: the client is ready to sign the deal. Men will start to finalize the sale as soon as they see a lull in the conversation. For example, when selling a life insurance policy, a man might say, "And your middle initial is?" as he starts the application and the deal closes. In contrast, a woman might take the positive feedback and foster the relationship by saying, "Have we addressed all of your needs?" and again, the deal closes. The fear from a male perspective is that you are opening yourself up for more questions. Although this portion of the sales process might take a little longer for women, you can see how in both instances, the deal would close, but one relationship would be long-term and one would not. Having said that, you don't want to be "Vicki Visitor" or "Tammy Timid." This is the time to finish the process—and your client *does* expect you to close the deal.

Scenario #2: Can We Have a Minute?

The second scenario is always a little trickier: the client has questions or needs privacy before closing the deal. Sometimes having to think about your product or service means they are asking for more information or perhaps just a little space for themselves. Other times it means they really need to think about it. Maybe it's your product or maybe it's their budget. When I was trained, sales associates were told that the way to handle this would be to say, "We have already discussed your budget and the product at length. Wouldn't you agree that making a decision that is so important to you should be done now?" If they still need more time, I was taught to respond, "I've gone over the product so that you understand it. It must be me then. Tell me what I did wrong so I can correct it next time." This approach often made the client feel uncomfortable and guilty. Many times the deal was closed, but often it was cancelled before the salesperson got home. I never used this tactic; however, some of the most successful men in my company included it as part of their scripting.

Going back to building relationships, at this point in the process, women are still asking questions. But, sometimes you just can't get to the root of the problem. Have you ever had to tell someone that you just met that you can't afford something? Isn't budget one of the hardest objections to overcome? When I was in the field and I came across the situation that they needed to think about it and I knew that all questions had been answered, all needs had been fulfilled and the price didn't seem to be a factor, I would excuse myself and give the clients a few minutes by themselves. Many times the wife would remind the husband what funds were available and when. These few minutes of privacy were sometimes all they needed to make the decision. Women listen hard—not just to what has been said, but what is *not* said.

Scenario #3: Another Time and Place

The third scenario is the most challenging: the client is not ready to close and needs more time. They will not make a decision after one meeting. The reaction to this was not favorable when I was trained. I was told, "Go out there, use what you have, let them buy you and don't come back without a check. If you don't close it after the first visit, someone is coming right behind you that will." I was told that was not a threat but rather an absolute guarantee.

My approach was a bit softer. I would tell my clients, "I understand this is such an important decision to make. Sometimes you need a little time to digest the information. Why don't we schedule an appointment for next week at this time, since this seems to have been a perfect time for us both? Between now and then, review the information and please call me with any questions that you have." Not only did I make my clients feel at ease, I quickly discovered who was serious about continuing the process and who was not. Those that did not schedule another appointment went into a different file and would be followed up with at a later date. Those that did schedule that next appointment felt confident with their decision and would refer me to their friends and families. When I shared my version of the appointment at my company, I was told "Don't be such a girl," and, "Grow up, or you will never be successful." But I was successful and my business was based solely on referrals after my first year. I built relationships and many of my clients have become friends. I proved that "being a girl" was a good idea.

Making a Lasting Impression
Even if you are in a sales job where you will only see your customer once, building a relationship is still important.

Being someone that your customer can count on goes a long way toward future business with them, as well as earning their trust with their referrals. By asking the right questions, listening attentively, and collaborating with your client to find a solution that fits their specific needs, you achieve a win-win for everyone. The client feels they have been heard—something that is especially important for women—and is confident in their decision to buy from you. Meanwhile, you close a sale built on integrity and respect.

In the next two chapters, we'll look at another key factor for building trust, and smart strategies for nurturing your client relationships over the long term that will put an end to cold calling forever.

SKIRT WISDOM

- Building a relationship builds trust and helps the client feel confident about their decision to buy.

- Fact-finding is the most effective way to lay the foundation for a long-term relationship.

- Use open-ended and approval questions to understand all of the client's needs and considerations.

- Set aside preconceptions and listen to what your client is really telling you.

- Exercise patience when asking and answering questions; the time you invest will be well worth it.

- If a client needs more time to think, get on their calendar before you leave.

- Closing the sale is part of the relationship.

CHAPTER FOUR

PRODUCT KNOWLEDGE

One of the keys to being successful in sales is knowing your product. Imagine going to sell someone your product or service and you knew nothing about the product itself or its features and benefits. Displaying your product knowledge to your customer is essential for building your credibility and your success. Each client you have is looking to you to become their trusted advisor and help guide them through the sales process. You are building a relationship through this trust.

Here are a few reasons why product knowledge is essential to successful sales:

Knowledge is power and product knowledge can mean more sales. It is difficult to effectively sell to a client if we cannot show how a particular product will address their needs. Women tend to be more detail-oriented and will help to provide solutions by asking questions. Men will want to solve the problem without offering the explanation of *why* this is the correct solution.

Knowledge will help you to be excited about your

product. Nothing is better than an excited salesperson that believes in their product and is able to provide solutions for their customer, because they understand what they are selling.

Knowledge helps you to become more confident. Many times a sale falls through because the client is not confident in the salesperson. Having the product knowledge, being able to show the features and benefits, and being able to translate those into simple terms will increase your own confidence as well as your client's confidence in you.

Knowledge helps to overcome objections. When you can anticipate an objection and address it upfront, it no longer is a concern.

This doesn't mean that you take all your product information and dump it onto your customer—if you do this, you'll get a deer-in-the-headlights look. This simply means that you should:

- Understand how the product works

- Describe what would happen if your customer had this product/service

- Describe what would happen if they *didn't* have the product/service

The more you know, the better you can help your customers. Your goal is to illustrate why your product or service is the one they should choose. At the same time, your customer is more interested in learning about how you're going to solve their problem than in hearing every nuance of the product. You want to let them know how your product or service will add the most value. And you can't show the value if you don't understand the product.

SKIRT TIP

Knowing your product empowers you to make an informed recommendation. You can explain how the product addresses the client's needs, rather than push for a sale that may not be in their best interest.

Know Your Resources

One major component of product knowledge involves knowing your resources. Have that information in your back pocket so that your customer doesn't need to know any other phone number but yours when it comes to your product or service. Make sure you know whom you can count on in other departments of your company. If you are a one-person show, know who you can call—perhaps a vendor, industry organization, or other resource—so that if a question comes up that you can't answer on the sales appointment, you can pick up the phone and get a quick response.

I had so many questions when I started in sales that I was nicknamed the "Question Queen." When I entered the office I would see eyes roll and the groaning would begin. My team knew I would have questions and many times I had questions the rest of the team hadn't thought of. In the long term, my questions were helpful to everyone. I started calling the home office and found out quickly not only who would respond to me immediately, but who actually had the correct information. So, while I didn't always have the answer to every customer question, I did always know how and where to find that answer.

Describe, Explain and Illustrate

Knowing your product also means being able to describe it so that the person you're with wants to learn more and gets involved in the sale itself. Get your customer's interest in your product in a way they will understand. There is more to knowing your product than knowing what the brochure and website show. There is also practical application that hopefully you will uncover or will be trained on. If not, you will need to come up with a few ideas on your own—and you may need to get creative!

Case in Point: Anticipating Questions

We had no formal training when I was starting out in sales, so I had to incorporate my own ideas. I used flash cards to test myself on the products on my own. I also played a game with other salespeople to reinforce what I was trying to learn. I would have a few salespeople sit in a circle with me. I would name a product and toss a soft ball. Once the ball was tossed to you, you had to catch it and describe the product. The next person to catch the ball would give a benefit of having that product. The next person would describe what would happen if they didn't have the product.

This proved to be a valuable exercise and in

no time our team understood the product and all its features and benefits. This became known as the "You Throw Like a Girl" game. The advantage to playing this game was that we not only knew the products but could also anticipate questions or concerns that might come up and address them in our fact-finding session. To me, that was a grand slam.

Part of describing and explaining your product effectively hinges on understanding the difference between features and benefits.

A *feature* is what something is or does. For example:

- A health insurance plan offers coverage for mammograms.

- A built-in rearview camera turns on automatically when the car is in reverse.

A *benefit* is why the feature is important, and what it means to the buyer. For example:

- By having coverage for mammograms, the client can detect breast cancer in its early stages and increase her chance of a complete recovery.

- By having a built-in rearview camera, the customer can back up more safely and reduce the risk of damaging the vehicle.

Men and women both buy benefits, not features. You need to go beyond simply stating the feature as the solution. You need to describe how it benefits your customer.

Know Your Customer—Then Your Product

Which do you think makes an effective salesperson: great knowledge of the product being sold or an understanding of the customer and the sales process? *It is more important to know your customer than it is to know your product.*

Okay, I realize that I am contradicting the point I just made about the value of knowing your product. But in the bigger picture, knowing every answer to every product question is not nearly as important as knowing your customer's needs and desires. Ultimately, the product information can be found in a manual or brochure. It's important to find the right solution for each customer. To get to the point of knowing your customer and determining what solution might work the best for the customer's needs, you need to build that relationship. Almost every aspect of the sales process is dependent on that premise. For women buyers, especially, you must take the time to cultivate the relationship rather than just solve the problem.

Imagine that you are just arriving home from work. Earlier in the day, you had an interesting business meeting that has sparked your thinking. When you walk in the door at home, you are eager to share with your significant other the details of the meeting and how it inspired you. You don't want them to interject with ideas and suggestions while you're in the middle of your story (although you may ask for their input once you're done). Nor are you that concerned with their understanding of the minutiae of the business or industry you're in, or the people involved with the meeting earlier that day. You really just want them to listen, so they understand the general context and your perspective on the issue. Your significant other's ability to understand you first, hear your ideas, and then offer feedback demonstrates a level of interest and commitment, which in turn foster trust and goodwill—both of which are integral to making the relationship work.

The same holds true when you are building relationships with your clients. The ability to explain specific features is important, but it's not nearly as critical as understanding the sales process, knowing how to read and react to different buying personality styles, and qualifying potential customers. We will go into different learning styles as well as different selling styles in a later chapter.

Know Your Product, But Don't Obsess Over Details
Many industries do not feel the need to provide you with product knowledge. You will find this in engineering and technical industries and some financial services, as well. There are "experts" out there that can speak the language and close the deal for you...or so I was told. I would hear, "Don't worry your pretty little head with all that information. The customer will buy you and that face, so you're good to go."

As flattering as I would like to say that is, remember, consumers are much savvier today than they were even 10 years ago. They have more information available to them in seconds, and often they will do their homework before you arrive.

I am sure that combining a product expert with a salesperson is sometimes easier than training someone else on product. Often this is evident with a female in a very technical male-dominated industry. I have been paired with a product expert and I have been trained on products so I could describe the features and benefits myself. In both cases I tried my best to learn as much as I could about the product so that I was able to understand it and explain it to my customer. The bottom line is you should be prepared—but don't wait to get out there until you are a pro at every facet of the business. Find those that have the product knowledge and spend some time asking questions. Find out the most commonly asked questions and have responses for those. Remember, analysis causes paralysis and you make no money sitting home for weeks and weeks studying.

Case in Point: Tap Resources to Win Confidence
I was recently in a large home improvement store looking for a particular item. I had trouble finding the item, so I asked a female associate whether she could help me locate it. She looked in numerous locations because she said that product would overlap into different categories. I was happy she knew that because I certainly did not. After looking everywhere possible, and with no luck, she suggested we go over to the special order desk where she would continue the search.

We did find what I was looking for and she

ordered it and had it shipped to my home to make it more convenient for me. She had spent about 30 minutes with me, which may not sound like a lot, but in that store it is. When we were done she asked whether there was anything else she could help me with and I told her that I do training for women who are in a male-dominated industry and wanted to ask a few questions. She agreed and here is what I found out:

Was there a training program? Yes, but mostly computer-based on products only. There was no training on customer service.

Who delivered the training? The instructions were given to her by someone who could explain about the online training process (the trainer happened to be male).

What were the expectations? You have 30 days to learn what you can and get out on the floor and 60 days to prove yourself or you are out the door. Any additional product training would be done on an associate's own time (and the store had more than 80,000 products).

I then asked whether she had any training on working with customers and she said no, but she felt that her job was to treat everyone the way she would want to be treated because that was what she learned growing up. Understanding your customer and their needs is part of building a relationship. I know if I ever need something for my home, I will be

SELLING IN A SKIRT

returning to that home improvement store because I have a new relationship with that sales woman.

Remember, people are buying solutions to their problems. If you don't know what that problem is, you can't solve it. Throughout the entire sales process, you should focus on understanding the client's needs, asking questions and reframing their answers for clarification, and thinking strategically to find the right solution. Although men may be satisfied by a checklist of features and benefits, women want more. Ultimately, they are buying *you*. The more you engage in a dialogue and build the relationship, the more they will trust you and feel confident following your recommendations. In the next two chapters, we will look at ways to nurture a relationship with a customer over time, so they not only become a repeat customer, but also pass along your information to others in their social circle as a reliable resource.

SKIRT WISDOM

- Product knowledge is essential in the consultative sales process and in building a relationship with the client.

- Aim to become a trusted resource for your client, and the only number they need to call.

- Know where to go for information if the client asks a question that you cannot answer.

- Explain the practical application and benefits of your product, not just the features.

- Remember to focus on the customer's needs and bringing solutions that address those problems.

SELLING IN A SKIRT

CHAPTER FIVE

THE TIES THAT BIND

Kim Duke, known in the industry as the "Sales Diva," emphasizes the importance of building relationships with clients in her e-book "The Five Biggest Sales Mistakes Women Make." In the book, Duke recounts a run-in she had with a client that her good ol' boy boss sent her to see. Being a fresh-faced newbie, Duke called on the client—a chef and upscale restaurateur—prepared to sell television ads. Her attitude changed from blind enthusiasm to total mortification as the client proceeded to rip her head off, spewing vitriol as he berated her company for its lack of customer service.

Although he apologized at the end of his rant, noting that Kim herself was not to blame, the writing was on the wall. Duke calmed the chef and promised to answer all of his questions, but when she got back to the office, she confronted her boss. Her boss—hidebound to the traditional way of doing business—had totally neglected to build a relationship with the client. After the initial sale, he moved on. And what happened? Despite Duke's best efforts to salvage the relationship, the chef never purchased another ad from her company.

Sound familiar? Depending on the industry you are in, you may only see a customer one time, or you may have the opportunity to nurture a longer relationship. If your line of business falls into the latter category— whether you are selling cars, computer networks, or insurance coverage—you should recognize that your client may have certain expectations after the sale.

SKIRT TIP

The relationship you established with a client during the initial sale won't last very long if you don't keep in touch and maintain a dialogue.

Often, sales associates will avoid any follow-up contact with a client for fear of doing or saying something that would cause the client to change their mind. On the other hand, the client, having made the decision to buy, may expect the salesperson to check in on them after the sale or provide ongoing service. Your goal is to build a strong, long-lasting client base, rather than engage in a series of short-term transactions. Keeping your client relationships going requires effort, but you can streamline those efforts so they don't become tedious.

Nurture the Relationship
Relationships have a one-on-one dynamic. Nobody wants to have a relationship with a company, they want

to connect with you as an individual. You want to be the person that the client thinks of when they have a particular need—or if they know someone who has a need you can fill. To become that go-to person, you've got to make the relationship feel personal.

When I worked in insurance sales, I used to keep a packet of thank you cards in my car. As soon as I left a meeting with a client, I would write a personal thank you note and send it from a mailbox around the corner. The client would receive my note the next day, and I would look like a hero for being so thoughtful.

I even recommend sending thank you cards to prospects when you don't close the sale. Sometimes the best referrals come from those you can't help with your product or service. They appreciate the fact that you took the time to sit with them and go over what is available, even if it's not for them, and they will tell their friends and colleagues what a pro you are.

Of course, one thank you card does not a relationship make. To nurture the connection over the long term, you need to keep the lines of communication open—and you need the communication to be authentic. Nobody likes to feel like they are just another contact in your customer relationship management system that you only call on when your sales numbers are down. The secret is to look for ways to reach out that have nothing to do with your product and everything to do with the client.

Another trick I developed early in my insurance sales career was to create a birthday card file for all of my clients. As soon as I would complete an application for a new client, I would write the client's name, address and date of birth on an index card. I kept all of the index cards in a recipe box file, organized by month. I would also create an index card for every member of the client's immediate family. Then, at the beginning of each month, I would pull all the index cards for that month and hand-write a birthday greeting.

In our technology-driven culture, you may be tempted to automate this process by sending an email greeting or e-card. I encourage you to go old school and stick with snail mail. Who doesn't feel extra special when they receive a hand-written birthday, anniversary or holiday card in the mail? That extra investment of a few hours can pay off huge dividends over time, especially in the form of referral business.

Be a Resource

Imagine no more cold calling. Imagine that your clients trust and appreciate you so much that they tell all of their friends and associates who share their need for your product or service. Imagine never having to find new business, but instead building your client base solely on referrals. Heaven!

A referral is the most expensive free lead. Why expensive? Because you have to invest the time into building and nurturing the relationship, and it's an exclusive lead—you're the only one that gets it. The "slam-bam-thank-you-ma'am" approach to sales doesn't win referrals. You are out of sight and out of mind for the client as fast as he or she is for you. To win referrals, you must win trust. To win trust, you must engage with the client on a deeper level, and be vested for the long term. To engage with the client, you must ask questions.

SKIRT TIP Want more referrals? Go above and beyond after the sale. Send a fruit basket to a new homeowner, or send a beautiful pen to the client who purchased a high-end PC. You can bet they will tell a dozen people about your kind gesture. If gifts are not permissible in your industry, simply continue to offer exceptional service to earn your customer's allegiance.

According to a study by Ogilvy and Mather, 92 percent of all women pass along information about deals or finds to others. How many others? Women have an average of 171 contacts in their email or mobile phone list, the study shows.

Case in Point: The Power of Referrals

In the heyday of my insurance sales career, I had an appointment with a woman who was a videographer. I walked into her office and she never even looked up. She told me to sit down and tell her what I had. I did the entire presentation to the top of her head and, although I recognized that she was busy, I admittedly thought she was pretty rude.

As I wrapped up by presentation and answered all of her initial questions, I asked her whether she had any other questions for me. She responded with, "Who do I make the check out to?"

Okay, maybe she wasn't that rude? But her head was still down and she was still concentrating on what she was writing. I finished filling out all the paperwork and she signed everything. As I thanked her, she looked up and said to me, "I bet you were thinking I was being rude."

Oops, did I say it out loud??

"What I was doing was making a list of the other videographers that I know that need to hear from you. I knew I could trust you from the moment you walked in the door. What I am going to do is give you this list but will call each one first and let them know that you will be contacting them. Is that ok?"

I thought I was on Candid Camera, and in short order, I had no need to prospect for clients.

Women also leverage social media to share information, with 53 percent of the female population (roughly 42 million women) participating in social media sites at least weekly, according to a 2009 survey by BlogHer, iVillage and Compass Partners. Just as noteworthy, 34 percent of women use social networks to get information, while 20 percent are looking for advice and recommendations.

If you want to gain access to a client's social network, you must first build a relationship with the client. For female customers, communication and relationship are key. Communicate with a woman effectively, and not only will she follow your recommendations, but she will be your biggest evangelist.

Remember, too, that when a woman makes a decision, she considers not only her own needs, but the impact on everyone around her—friends, family, and associates. You cannot see the bigger picture if you don't ask the right questions and keep probing to understand all of the factors that will weigh into her decision-making process.

SKIRT TIP
If you own your own business, regardless of the industry, you can use social networking tools to build and nurture relationships with clients and prospects. The key is not to sell, but rather be a resource for useful information.

Trust takes effort to earn, but it pays off in huge dividends down the road. Once you have listened effectively to a client's needs, answered her questions, and earned the handshake, you have a client for life. Not only that, but your client's extended network of friends, relatives, and acquaintances will get your recommendation, too. By investing the extra time now, you can eventually pave the way for a future free of prospecting.

Case in Point: These Boots Were Made for Walkin'

Back in the early 1990s, cell phone plans were analog, not digital, and my bill averaged about $2000/month. No one had my cell phone number except my children and my office. Everyone else had my home office number, because I didn't want my bill to be higher than it was, so you have a good idea of how much I was on the phone.

One Friday in June, I had to confirm one of my three appointments for that Saturday. The prospect was very hard to reach originally but agreed to an appointment, *if* I confirmed at 3:00 p.m. on Friday... so I did. He asked me why I was coming to see him and I said, "Because you need to know me." That is how we left it.

I finished my first appointment on Saturday and was in my car en route to the hard-to-reach client when my phone rang. It was my son, and I had a sense that he was not delivering good news. He told me that the client that I confirmed with the day before had called to cancel. That didn't sit well with me, so I called the client and asked why he would cancel our appointment before he even met me. He explained that he was laying a foundation for a construction project and his laborers didn't show, so he had to go to the job site and would not be near his office.

Not one to be swayed by circumstance, I asked where the job site was and told him that I would be right near there. He laughed and said that I would never show up, and I laughed and said, "I'll meet you there." Of course, I was not dressed for a job site, but I always have a pair of workboots in my car. (To this day I still do, by the way.)

I showed up at the job site before he arrived and waited until he showed up. He said he liked my spunk and we proceeded to do the appointment from the hatchback of my car. He liked everything I had to say and then informed me that he had to think about it and that I should come back on Wednesday. I looked at him and said, "Really? What other questions can I answer? What other information do you need?" He reminded me that his checkbook was in the office, and he had not been by there yet that day.

So, on Wednesday I showed up on the job site and I wrote policies for his family and his brother's family. He told me to come back the following Wednesday and to just bring applications. I did and consequently wrote all of the men on his construction crew. In truth, his guys had no idea what they were buying, but he told them he trusted me and that they should do business with me. After that he referred me to the framers, the plumbers, the electricians, and practically every other team that worked on the construction project. I received referrals for months and I didn't have to search for prospects.

Earlier I made the point about how using the female-centric method of sales and relationship-building can increase your success rate with female clients. As the above story illustrates, the same strategy is often highly effective with male clients, as well. Although men are more inclined to bypass friendly banter and cut to the chase when making a purchasing decision, they still appreciate a sales professional who will go the extra mile and take their individual needs into consideration to find the right solution.

SKIRT TIP

Although male customers may not be naturally inclined to engage in discourse, asking fact-finding questions and building rapport often is just as effective with men as with women.

In the next few chapters, we will look at ways that the female-centric communication style can affect women's professional development in the sales industry—in both good ways and bad. We will also explore strategies for cultivating saleswomen's inherent strengths during training, while navigating the sometimes complex communication issues and rivalries that can develop between male and female associates in the workplace.

SKIRT WISDOM

- It takes extra time to build a relationship, but it is definitely worth the investment.

- Creating easy-to-use systems to reach out to clients can make you look like a hero with little extra effort.

- If you are a resource to your clients, you will be top-of-mind when they need to buy again.

- Remember that women love to share information. Whether or not you get the sale, a prospect may provide referrals.

- Referrals are exclusive leads—you are the only one to get the information, and it's incumbent upon you to nurture that new relationship.

SELLING IN A SKIRT

Part Three
PROFESSIONAL DEVELOPMENT

SELLING IN A SKIRT

CHAPTER SIX

TAILORED TRAINING

Many companies have not discovered the strength females bring to the sales force. Other businesses grasp that women are "naturals" but then want to train all the "naturalness" out of them by forcing them to use the (formerly successful) more male-centric sales techniques. As a result, female sales associates often face a dilemma: they understand that they have an ability to build strong relationships—yet they are trained that the "right" way is aggressive, with a quick close.

Many traditionally male-dominated companies still use the old analogy of sales as a "war." When I invited my readers to share their stories on my blog, I received an email from one woman who worked for one of the top communications companies in the world. Her boss, one of the company presidents, decided to play the song "Eye of the Tiger" from the soundtrack to *Rocky III* every morning to pump up the staff. He spoke constantly about waking up in the morning, ready for combat. He pressured his staff to "crush" and "kill" the enemy. Do you think that he promoted an environment that motivated everyone who worked for him? Do you think that the training she received encouraged her to employ her own unique talents as a woman to succeed?

SKIRT TIP
Research shows that men tend to be competitive, whereas women are collaborative. Sales leaders should develop training and motivational strategies that speak to both genders for the best results.

To compete in the modern economy, companies need a training program tailored to women's strengths. That does not mean each company needs a separate training program for women, nor does it mean changing the entire program to focus on women as sales professionals and as buyers. But what companies must do is ensure that the training program explains and embraces both styles of communication—the "Voice-Male" and "Voice-Female" dynamic. This will empower sales professionals to work within their strengths rather than employ a cookie-cutter approach with every client.

Power Plays

Conflicts can arise during training before the topic of customer relations is ever broached. In fact, from the very first meeting, trainers may witness tensions between male and female sales associates. Why? Women are comfortable asking for help—a trait that men can view as a weakness.

Women tend to ask a lot of questions before they

start a task, whereas men roll up their sleeves and dive right in. A woman's inclination to verify and validate information provides her the confidence and knowledge to perform well; however, men will interpret this tendency to deliberate as a sign of reluctance or inability. If they were up to the job, men reason, the women wouldn't ask so many questions.

Ironically, such crossed wires can create obstacles in a woman's career that are not of her own doing, but rather caused by others' interpretation of her actions. In *Talking from 9 to 5: Women and Men at Work*, Dr. Deborah Tannen shares the account of a medical doctor who, during her medical training, received a low grade from her supervising physician. Knowing that she was one of the best interns in her group, she was baffled. Upon asking her supervisor for an explanation, she learned that because she asked so many questions, her supervisor assumed that she didn't know the material as well as her peers. The male doctor had interpreted her learning style as a negative, rather than recognizing it as evidence that she was more engaged in the material than the other interns.

Rather than ignoring or deflecting questions— much less assuming that the person asking them is a slow learner—trainers should acknowledge and answer questions as time permits. Doing so demonstrates that women's inquisitive approach is valid and can also foster more dialogue between participants. The training still can be very structured while allowing opportunities for engagement and interaction, which help cultivate the sense of relationship that female sales associates value. At the same time, male associates can benefit from learning the answers to questions they might not be as willing to ask.

SKIRT TIP
Taking questions from sales associates during training can open up a dialogue among team members, keeping them engaged in the material and adding new insights to the standard curriculum.

The Mind's Eye

Another area in which gender-specific communication styles can cause challenges is in the use of illustrations and metaphors. Women frequently use anecdotes related to the home or relationships—saying something is "like cleaning the house while the kids are still growing" or "the cherry on top"—whereas men draw analogies to the sport arena and the battlefield with quips like, "We slaughtered our competitor" or "I really hit it out of the park." Why are these metaphors a problem? Well, the opposite gender may not understand or recognize the meaning behind your illustration. For example, a woman may not understand what a man means when he says, "We had to move the goalposts." If a woman likens a facet of one deal to the "icing on the cake," a man may be baffled—isn't frosting just that thick, gooey extra stuff that should be scraped off? Such misunderstandings can lead to frustration for all parties involved. In some ways, men and women are speaking different languages, and any dialogue they share may be abruptly cut short with the wrong analogy.

The solution? Trainers can draw attention to this crucial difference as part of the training program, illustrating the need to modify language based on whether the client is a man or woman. Doing so will also raise awareness among participants that the same rules apply in the workplace, as well. In addition, don't simply gender-reverse images in your communication. Instead, try to incorporate gender-neutral images—for example, something related to nature or the weather—or paraphrase the illustration and explain what you mean to ensure that the analogy will hit home with both genders.

Double Duty

More and more businesses are becoming mindful of the need to modify sales training to speak to women buyers. Countless others have yet to make this leap. Their training programs still focus on transactional selling versus the consultative approach. Be prepared—as a woman working in sales, you may find yourself learning everything twice: your trainer's way and your way. That's okay. Remember that your goal is not to completely adapt to one way of dealing with a client, or to adopt methods of selling that are completely foreign to the way you think. Instead, your goal is to find a way to work within the parameters that you have been given, using your own unique talents and strengths. If that means altering your techniques after your training is done so that your approach feels natural, then go for it!

Case in Point: Phoning It In

When I was going through my initial sales training in the insurance field, I was given the telephone schedule that was used by all the top producers. Our success was dependent on the appointments that we set for ourselves. On my first day of training, I was handed a script and given a spot to sit in. I decided to listen for a bit so I could get the juices flowing. I soon noticed that everyone was loud and no one was given the "right of way" to make a call. If you picked up the phone, you soon found yourself practically shouting at the person whose number you dialed just to be heard.

What's more, the sales approach felt very counterintuitive. I could already tell this style was not for me. I heard what other sellers were saying to their prospects:

"Let me explain the plan."

"You will need to give me a check."

"If everything looks good we will be writing an application."

"When was the last time you were hospitalized and for what?"

"What medications do you take?"

I certainly wouldn't give that kind of personal information to someone I didn't know; yet, I was told that we needed to acquire this information on the phone *before* the appointment. I was also told that I shouldn't go on an appointment unless I was going to be picking up a check—plain and simple.

"Why waste your time? What if the person doesn't qualify?" my trainer asked me. And my favorite statement from the trainer: "Don't be such a girl by trying to make friends with everyone."

Initially, my schedule went something like this:
Morning meeting – 8:00 a.m. to 10:00 a.m.
Phones – 10:30 a.m. to 9:00 p.m.

If I scheduled enough appointments on Monday, I didn't come back to make calls on Tuesday. If I didn't reach my quota, Tuesday was a shorter day of calls. I was (and am) a woman who thrives on building relationships—and sitting in a call center for days, making call after call, hardly qualifies as building a relationship. Being face-to-face with someone and listening to them is what I do best. I was determined to figure out a way to make that happen. I lasted on Monday until about 1:00 p.m.

The idea of being on the phone for so many hours just didn't make sense to me. So, I told my sales leader that I needed a quieter environment and that I would have the 20 appointments per week that were required—just not from the office. I was excused, with the caveat that if I didn't have the 20 appointments I would either be back in the office calling or I would be out of the job. After that, I never showed up at the office with less than 20 appointments.

I also didn't qualify anyone over the phone, yet was in front of more people and wrote more business by building relationships and receiving referrals from clients I went to see in person. I had discovered that my system worked—but my sales leader didn't think the system could be duplicated by others. I was fighting an uphill battle with no support.

Ladies, you are faced with finding a balance between your own style and the mandates of your manager and work environment. When coping with a trainer who wants the "relationship strength" you offer, but who wants to force you into the "right" technique, keep this in mind:

- Own your emotions. Giving way to over-the-top emotional reactions is considered unprofessional and will impede your ascent at work. Instead, vent in private.

- Find ways to challenge your boss or trainer without appearing disrespectful.

- Figure out what your trainer is missing or doesn't understand.

- Try it the "traditional" way, but remember to try it "your way," too.

- Don't be afraid to use your inherent relationship-building skills.

Remember that although sales force leaders acknowledge that women offer strong company client relationships, old habits are hard to break. All too often, trainers teach women to bypass their strengths to get straight to the close. Discovering how to walk that tightrope will help you to succeed using your own special skill set.

SKIRT TIP

Sales managers who keep an open mind about communication styles may discover that a different sales approach can be more effective for some associates.

Ladies First

We already know that women are behind 85 percent of all purchases and that the way women approach buying decisions is very different from men. Women shop, men buy. Women scan, men look for a specific item. In short, women are gatherers and men are hunters. Sales training programs should acknowledge these differences.

Does this mean creating two separate courses of training—one geared for women and another for men? No, but until more companies recognize the need to alter their programs from a transactional to a consultative approach, trainers will need to supplement traditional training methods with a module designed for engaging both female sales consultants and female clients. This doesn't have to be an elaborate process; instead, trainers should encourage their associates to modify their approach if they are selling to a woman instead of a man.

There should be no "one size fits all" approach to

sales. Any training program should cover fundamental strategies for engaging the client, answering questions and closing the sale. But in the big picture, sales associates should be encouraged to use the approach that comes most naturally to them. Rather than forcing everyone into a mold, trainers can inspire their salespeople to use their own unique strengths and talents to close the sale. This model of training, quite different from what was considered the standard for decades, will give sales associates of either gender the confidence to go out and blaze a new trail.

Relationships Are Key

In the same way that sales professionals of both genders can sell more effectively to women by building a relationship with the customer, managers can train more effectively by focusing on relationships. In the context of sales training, that means asking questions of participants during training to learn their desires and expectations using the same fact-finding approach as you would at the initial meeting with a new client. Women (and men) should be encouraged to share their opinions and draw on personal experience in discussing sales training topics.

Saleswomen and male sales managers who work together to identify ways to incorporate the most effective relationship-building techniques the entire team can use often will resolve some of the battle-of-the-sexes tension that can surface between associates of the opposite gender. At the same time, by using open-ended questions and other relationship-building strategies as part of the sales training process, managers can demonstrate their effectiveness to the participants, who can then adopt the technique when communicating with prospective clients.

In the next chapter, we will look at ways women can leverage relationship-building tools, like social media, to find new job opportunities, and how they can best set themselves up for success in the workplace. Then, we will explore ways that sales force leaders can use their understanding of women's decision-making process and communication style to attract and retain talented female sales associates for the benefit of their business.

SKIRT WISDOM

- Effective sales training acknowledges and embraces the difference in the way men and women learn and communicate.

- Female sales professionals should be encouraged to ask questions, but should also respect the position of their sales leader.

- When illustrating a point, choose gender-neutral references for metaphors and analogies.

- As a woman in sales, your goal is to adapt the sales approach learned in training to your unique strengths.

- Fact-finding to build relationships is as important in sales training as it is when speaking with a customer.

CHAPTER SEVEN
RISING IN THE RANKS

Before you can develop your career as a sales professional, you first need to land the job. The good news is that the growing use of social media plays to women's natural strengths and can make the job hunt more smooth and enjoyable than it may have been in previous years.

Social media has shifted the hiring process and the workplace environment more toward a consultative setting and away from a transactional one. In other words, the working environment is now geared toward a woman's strength of creating relationships, rather than the male strength of completing the transaction. But, just because building relationships comes easily doesn't mean that the job search is a cake walk. To get the job you really want, you must be assertive in your approach.

Getting the Interview
The first step to landing a plum position is to interview with the companies you hope will hire you. Today, employers and candidates no longer rely on newspaper ads or job

boards to find the right match. Instead, often they reach out to friends and colleagues through social media sites, like LinkedIn, Plaxo and even Facebook, to get the word out. Likewise, they will tell friends and colleagues what they need and look to make the right connections. What does this mean for prospective job seekers? Getting the interview is all about *networking.*

Networking is not as formal as it sounds. It is simply calling everyone you know, telling them what you want— in this case, a job—and asking them for advice on how to get it. The hard part will be swallowing your pride. The next hardest part will be contacting everyone you know to tell them that you'd like 15 minutes of their time to get some career advice.

In short, networking is all about telling the people in your network what you want and asking whether they can help, or whether they know anyone who can help. That action is what turns your network into a verb: networking. The key is to be focused and active in your search.

For women, the new paradigm of job hunting through friends and business associates plays to our inherent strengths. Successful networking depends on having rich, deep relationships. The strength of men is their ability to close the deal. Keep this in mind when you are networking: women are relational, men are transactional. When building your relationships with other women, make sure you actually ask for what you need. Likewise, when dealing with men, you can do some relational chatting, but know that behind that smile, they are thinking, "Why am I here? What does she want?" Be sure you get to the point as soon as possible.

SKIRT TIP Looking for a new job? Fill your social calendar. Schedule coffee dates and lunch meetings with people in your network who can help connect you to prospective employers, and use the time to nurture those relationships while also gathering the information you need.

Once you are in the networking process, remember that your goal is get an interview. Ask the questions that will uncover how the people in your network can help you find that job. For example, ask whether they know anyone who is doing that sort of job now who might give you an "informational interview". Or maybe they know someone in a related job, or can recommend an organization you can join that would connect you to the right people.

Once you find people in your network with the right connections, use the same fact-finding technique that you would with a sales client. Ask questions about the culture of a company, the pros and cons of the specific tasks you would do, the benefits and salary ranges you can expect to encounter, or anything else that will strongly influence your decision.

Winning over a Prospective Employer

Armed with the background information you need, you are now looking for people who can actually interview you. The key to a successful job interview is feeling comfortable and confident that you *want* the job and that you *deserve* the job. You do not want to go in with the attitude that they are doing you a favor to hire you. (Trust me, no one hires out of pity.)

If the hiring manager does not believe you add value to the company or organization, you will not be hired, period. Before you go in for the interview, figure out what value you add, and own it throughout the process. You should always be truthful, and you can include important facts and figures to support your case, such as years worked and where, grade point average, number of people you've supervised, etc. Stories from previous jobs or projects can help you to illustrate the skills you bring to the table. Keep in mind, however, that women are relational, men transactional, and adjust the amount of detail you include in your stories accordingly.

Don't be shy about asking the questions you need to understand whether the company and the job would be a good fit for you. You have your intel from your networking—use it! A male interviewer likely will be looking to close the deal quickly and will want to answer your questions in such a way as to help you make the final decision. Therefore, it would help you to explain why you want to know the answer when talking to male interviewers. With female interviewers, on the other hand, you can ask more "what if" scenarios and open-ended questions that help you see how the job would fit into your life, and how you can contribute to the company.

Also, be aware of body language throughout the interview. Again, the genders do not communicate the same way. When male managers meet with their female counterparts, they inadvertently give off body signals that contradict their words, leading to a disconnect between the two. For example, when men listen to other men, they are often shoulder-to-shoulder and may not even look at each other. Men typically have minimal or limited eye contact with each other. They typically don't nod their head or respond with comments while listening. Men both deliver, and listen for, facts and figures. In contrast, women tend to face each other, and they trust people who look them in the eye. We participate in the conversation and, as a result, we want that contribution acknowledged.

SKIRT TIP

Don't take a male interviewer's avoidance of eye contact or lack of affirming gestures as signs of disinterest. Men are generally very data driven and do not reveal their thoughts through body language the way that women do.

As the interview winds up, you should take note of the final difference between men and women: Men want to decide now; women mull over their choices. This means it will be easier to explain to a woman that you want to take some time to make your decision. A male interviewer may take this delayed decision as a sign of disinterest or indecision on your part. Therefore, it would be best if you put a deadline on your decision, such as telling him that you'll call him by the end of the week.

The Uphill Climb

Once you land that plum position, you still have to navigate the complex communication landscape to gain solid footing for your career growth. More women are entering the sales force today than ever before; yet, women often face a double standard in sales. Frequently, they have to work twice as hard to overcome stereotypes and lingering prejudices just so they can achieve the same goal as their male peers.

For years, sales has been seen as a "man's game," with a strong focus on one-upsmanship and competition versus collaboration. Some men feel that using gentle persuasion and feminine instincts is trading on sexuality. Nothing could be further from the truth. In fact, a woman's inherent qualities of empathy, patience, and inquisitiveness are tremendously helpful in a sales environment.

If women have the right skill set for sales, why do they face such challenges in being recognized for their work?

Achieving gender equality in the workplace—whether in sales or any other industry—remains an uphill battle. Sadly, women can unknowingly hold themselves back by either attempting to step into a man's shoes, or by overtly flaunting their feminine wiles. More often than not, these tactics amount to shooting oneself in the foot.

His Way or the Highway No More

In the introduction to her book *Selling is a Woman's Game*, sales trainer Nicki Joy notes that women have a number of inherent gifts, including compassion, patience, endurance, talkativeness, tolerance, and resourcefulness, among others. Ironically, these traits are often frowned upon in a sales environment and perceived as signs of weakness or as hindrances to effective transactional selling. Female associates frequently feel frustrated by training programs that take a customer-as-conquest approach to sales and find themselves going against their gut instincts in an attempt to adapt to what is often a male-centric sales model.

SKIRT TIP

Because women are all about connecting, they can feel slighted or lose confidence when male colleagues demonstrate a competitive attitude.

Similarly, a female sales representative or manager may face being "left out of the loop" because she isn't part of the Boys Club at the office. She may have to endure occasional verbal slights and minor exclusions, which can be demoralizing and cause mounting tension in the workplace.

On my blog, I invited women to write in with their stories about working in a traditionally male-dominated industry. One story illustrates the boys' club mentality perfectly:

> Since I have been in the home construction industry for over 15 years, I have many stories

related to the guys that I now lovingly call "Bubbas." Unfortunately, most of them deal with some sort of gender discrimination; it still stuns me that many of the men in our industry don't get it yet!

One of these stories is from a year ago and the male involved was under the age of 40. His daddy owned the company that we both worked for and he did not like the fact that I was there; I always was reminded that his father was the owner! He had been treating me in a particularly rude and obnoxious way for a couple of weeks, so following a meeting, he asked that I remain in the conference room and he closed the door. We did work together often, so I was not surprised by the request. He proceeded to explain to me that he knew he was not being very agreeable and gave me the reason—he "was not getting enough sex at home from his wife." I was not able to escape, so I listened to the sordid details and reasons that he felt he had to mistreat me! I suggested that he get some counseling and finally was able to leave the room!

No, I did not file any complaint, but oddly enough, I was terminated just a few months later, after being there less than a year!

Is it possible to coexist as a female professional alongside members of the Boys' Club? Of course. Many women have done so for decades. It helps to know how to identify the good ol' boys mentality so that you can recognize it when you see it—and then formulate ways to work both within and outside of the framework so your career can continue to grow.

Here are a few antiquated methods that good ol' boys use—and expect everyone else to use as well:

- Use a "turn and burn" mentality to continually refill their sales pipeline without nurturing relationships.

- Rely on cold-calling instead of earning referrals to bring in new business.

- Focus more on making their sales quota than on solving a client's problem.

- Barrage prospects with a litany of features and benefits that don't address their specific needs.

- Use high-pressure sales tactics to coerce prospects into a buying decision.

- Bore customers with stories that aren't relevant to the situation.

As a woman in a traditionally male-dominated industry, you may feel a great deal of pressure to subscribe to these worn-out notions. Does this mean you have to submit to them in order to get ahead? Absolutely not. Take what you can from these techniques and then move forward in your career by using your own unique gifts. Doing so can be a delicate balancing act, so you will have to steel yourself for the inevitable tensions that may arise between the pressure to use traditional sales techniques and the desire to follow your own instinct.

Despite these frustrations, women today have an excellent opportunity to get ahead in sales by embracing their innate skills and by understanding the differences between male and female styles of communication.

SKIRT TIP

Choosing a career in sales may mandate that you develop a thick skin to deal with male colleagues, but don't lose your innate virtues of empathy and compassion. Those traits will serve you well when selling to female customers.

Speaking a New Language

In the same way that salesmen can improve their success rate by learning how women make buying decisions, female sales professionals can improve their career prospects by learning to adapt to men's communication styles in the workplace. Many women make the mistake of trying to be more assertive to hold their own with their male peers and managers, and instead come off as aggressive and pushy. To put it bluntly, you don't have to be a bitch to be successful in sales.

In his seminars for business professionals, psychologist and speaker Bruce Christopher explains the differences between "Voice Male" and "Voice Female" communication styles. Women tend to use an interpersonal style that draws on background and context to present ideas and information in a narrative fashion. They generally give a linear account of an event or thought process with lots of details and deliver the bottom line at the end of the story. For women, Christopher notes, the joy is in the telling of the story.

Men, on the other hand, can be downright agitated by such storytelling. In the 'Voice Male,' men do not speak in paragraphs, they speak in bullet points. They use shorter, clipped phrases to report information or thoughts without a lot of detail. More importantly, the bottom line does not come last, but first. Sometimes, the bottom line is all they will share, without the historical context or narrative that women desire. Not surprisingly, this communication style can be just as frustrating to women as the storytelling approach is to men.

As a woman in sales, you can improve your communication with your male peers by switching into "Voice Male" mode, when appropriate, and giving the bottom line first, then asking if they want more details. As Christopher notes, delivery is everything, and how you say something often is more important than what you are saying. Given the different communication styles, you also should not take it personally if a male coworker or manager seems to be curt or interrupts and asks for the bottom line in the middle of a conversation. It's not you, it's him.

Forward-thinking businesses often find ways to modify processes and tactics, making them more female-friendly. We'll look at some of these training strategies in the next chapter. Outside of any formal training program, however, women in sales can facilitate this transition by learning to use both male and female styles of communication and embracing those differences to achieve greater goals as a team.

Asserting Yourself with Grace

As men and women adjust to working together harmoniously in this brave new world, women may try to assume some male characteristics that they feel will bring success. These traits can be confusing to them, as well as to the men around them.

Men tend to be seen as "aggressive"—and that is an acceptable approach for men. When women try to mimic an aggressive attitude, they are often seen as overdoing it. Such an attitude is usually not well received. Women are stuck between a rock and a hard place trying to be ambitious without coming off as difficult or bitchy. According to Deborah M. Kolb, author of *Her Place at the Table: A Woman's Guide to Negotiating the Five Key Challenges to Leadership Success,* "To be a leader you have to be decisive and take charge. That fits fine for men, but when women do it they get labeled."

Women need not be aggressive. Instead, they can be assertive. Being assertive is the ability to communicate one's ideas or thoughts openly and with confidence. Acting in an *assertive* manner eliminates the forceful, in-your-face attitude that is usually associated with being "aggressive."

Case in Point: Asserting Yourself with Grace

My first sales leader was a woman who was clearly trying to mimic some of the traits of a fellow sales leader, who was a man. She was aggressive to the point of being abusive. When she wanted something done, she demanded it and there was not one bit of femininity in her entire persona or in any of the selling skills she was trying to teach. She made a point of letting everyone know she was performing like the male sales leader and that she would beat him in every contest in which they would compete. Interestingly, his behavior was just as aggressive as her behavior—but people tolerated it because he was male.

One day during our meeting I asked a question that I thought would be beneficial for her entire team. No sooner had I posed the question than she became irate and yelled, "IN MY OFFICE, NOW!" in front of more than 60 people. I walked into her office and she slammed the door, then proceeded to scream at me at the top of her lungs for a good five minutes. I knew everyone could hear every word. She accused me of making others feel as if she weren't doing her job because I had a question, snapping, "Why do you need to ask so many questions? Can't you just figure things out yourself? Couldn't you just get to the bottom line? You are acting like such a brat and such a girl."

She couldn't believe I dared to make her look bad in front of her male counterpart. And *that* was what truly bothered her—because no one ever questioned him. At the end of her tirade, I walked out of her office, walked past the stone-silent group, got in my car and drove home.

Unfortunately, I was driving a bit above the speed limit and was pulled over by a state trooper. His words to me were, "Honey, do you know how fast you were going?" I certainly was not going to challenge him about anything or question the way he spoke to me, because I still believed I should be respectful and have a positive attitude—even during this horrible day. He was kind enough to give me a warning (a $350 warning!) and sent me on my way.

A man likely would have dealt with a day like this by himself, following the "fight or flight" mentality and doing something physical, like hitting a few dozen balls at the driving range. Men are less likely to internalize these types of events or blow a gasket. Women do, which is why often we feel the need to "vent." As a woman, I could have gone home and told my children what happened so that I would feel loved and supported, but I decided to take a different route.   I drove back to work, walked into my manager's office, and handed him the speeding ticket. I told him bluntly that I was not paying this ticket and that the way the sales leader spoke to me was inappropriate and he would need to see how this could be changed. In this case, I was assertive—not aggressive. He took the ticket and brought me into the sales leader's office and told her not only was she going to pay the ticket, she was to buy me a radar detector. He added flatly that her aggressive behavior would stop then and there, and told her that she had not won this round. The conversation was short and sweet—the way the sales leader preferred—and my manager even added the sports metaphor to make his point.

Making your voice heard does not mean silencing everyone around you. Whether you are a man or a woman, being an effective leader does not mean being a bully. To further your sales career, building respectful relationships and understanding that men and women communicate differently is just as important in the workplace as it is with your clients.

SKIRT TIP

Asserting your own position and speaking with authority does not mean you have to throw others under the bus. Balance assertiveness with listening skills to ensure others feel heard.

Ask and Ye Shall Receive

On the other end of the spectrum, female sales professionals often are hesitant to ask questions outside of a training scenario, and their failure to speak up can hinder their career growth. Rather than ask for the recognition they deserve—which they view as being boastful or pushy—women instead will wait passively for others to recognize their contributions and achievements. According to Carnegie Mellon economist Linda Babcock, women are simply less likely to ask for higher salaries, better working conditions, or promotions than their male counterparts. In her book *Women Don't Ask: Negotiation and the Gender Divide,* Babcock recounts the story of a manager who, when asked why only his male employees received promotions, answered simply, "The women don't ask."

Learning when and how to ask the right questions is a delicate balancing act for most women. Although you may feel comfortable asking questions to get more information during a sales call, you might not be comfortable asking your boss for a raise.

As a sales professional, it will fall on you to learn how to ask the right questions at the right times to promote your career. Andrew Finlayson, author of *Questions That Work*, offers three simple steps to ask for what you need:

- Determine what you want to accomplish

- Consider how best to get your message across

- Prepare your questions in advance

By formulating your questions around these guidelines, you should be able to get directly to the heart of the matter, whether you are questioning your sales leader about specific training methods or preparing to ask your supervisor for flex time.

Reining in Your Emotions

I believe one of the wonderful qualities that women possess is their willingness to express their emotions.

Men will often stifle their feelings, whether joy or sadness, whereas women are comfortable sharing their feelings openly. This trait also tends to make women more compassionate toward others and manifests itself in complementary qualities, such as patience and adaptability. In the workplace, this expressiveness means that often women:

- More readily accept criticism and rectify behavior

- Are not shy about asking for advice or guidance

- Are able to admit when they are wrong

- Wait for their turn to talk during meetings

- Are well-prepared and pay attention to details

These are all admirable traits. Yet, as women, we sometimes need to modify our behavior in light of the bigger picture. For example, at the start of a team meeting, a female sales associate might offer to get coffee for a couple of her male coworkers. Suddenly, she has put herself in the role of hostess and subordinate rather than their equal, tacitly suggesting that she is more likely to take orders than give them.

SKIRT TIP

In the workplace, don't let your tendency toward being politely deferential keep you in the shadows. Ask for what you want, and claim your place at the table.

The desire to please and serve others—a sign of women's innate gravitation toward forming lasting relationships—can also lead them to cry easily and unexpectedly. Crying is a natural release to feelings that arise in our lives, particularly in high-stress situations. For a woman, that can include a situation in which she feels challenged or confronted, or one in which she recognizes that she is unprepared. Sometimes a woman will cry because she is angry or frustrated, and the default is to release tears in place of rage. Regardless of the scenario, crying in the workplace generally is viewed as inappropriate and unprofessional.

A woman can also be passed over for a promotion if she cries in front of her coworkers or boss. Men can't handle when women cry. Some may naturally want to hug or comfort them, but that is not appropriate. Others simply want to run to another office to get away from the tears. In both cases, they determine that the woman is too emotional to be an effective leader or manager. Both men and women in leadership believe that crying demonstrates incompetence or the inability to handle difficult situations.

Case in Point: The No Crying Rule

A few years ago, I was in an operations meeting being led by the vice president of our company. She was a no-nonsense type of leader who had a very firm hand. During the course of the meeting, she learned that a task she had assigned to a young manager in her late 20s—we'll call her Victoria—had not been done to the vice president's standards. She started in on her, and very soon I could see Victoria begin to panic. Tears were welling up in her eyes, and she literally started to hyperventilate. In short, she had a complete meltdown in front of her boss and had to excuse herself from the meeting to pull herself together.

After the meeting adjourned, Victoria was hysterically upset the entire time, berating herself for her performance on the task and for breaking down under pressure. I tried to console her, but I already knew what was coming.

Later that day, I spoke with the vice president, who informed me that she would never trust Victoria with a challenging assignment, because it was obvious that she could not handle any type of stress or criticism. I felt bad for Victoria, because she had great potential. Sadly, though, she likely will never move forward in her career because of her inability to rein in her emotions.

So how should women deal with this problem? When you feel yourself in a situation that will push you to the point of losing control of your emotions, remove yourself from the situation as quickly as possible. You need to act naturally but remain in control. Briefly excuse yourself and step into your office or into the restroom—anywhere that you can gather yourself and regain your composure. Being overly emotional will harm your credibility; however, your ability to be empathetic with others is integral to building relationships with your customers, especially other women. You want to keep your emotions under control in the workplace and channel them into relationship-building.

SKIRT TIP

The same sensitivity and genuine care that makes women effective in sales can backfire if left unchecked.

As women, we also have a tendency to take rejection personally, which can make it even harder to keep your emotions in check in a professional environment. Developing a thick skin can be difficult, but once you learn that being told "no" doesn't mean you are a lousy salesperson or a terrible loser, you can free yourself from constant emotional upheaval at work. I recently heard a story from another highly respected woman in the sales industry who used to drive to a local graveyard near her office after lunch every day so she could simply have a good cry. She was just starting out in sales and she found it difficult to manage objections from her clients. Even as she struggled, however, she recognized that it was better to take her emotions out of the office and give full vent to them in privacy until she could get herself under control. In time, the need to have a daily cry passed because she learned not to take every bump in the road as a reflection of herself as a person.

Dressing for Success

Talking about fashion choices in a book on sales strategies may seem off-topic, but the truth is that appearances matter. With more and more women in the workplace, and many heading for the corner office, it's important to be respected and taken seriously. From the time we were growing up, most girls played dress up. We graduated from princesses to pop stars and then we had our own style that would reflect how the world saw us. Dressing professionally isn't about *what* you wear—it's more about *how* you wear it.

When women first began joining the ranks of male-centric industries, there was an unspoken rule that they needed to dress like men in order to be taken seriously. Remember those "power suits" of the 1980s, with the outrageously padded shoulders? Did you ever see the movie *Big Business* with Bette Midler and Lily Tomlin? They played two sets of twins, separated at birth. One pair had gone on to become big, high-powered executives in New York; the other twins were simple country girls. When did the country cousins get to be taken seriously in the boardroom? When they discarded their frilly dresses and wore power suits with big chunky tennis shoes to work. How about Diane Keaton in *Baby Boom*? Her high-necked blouses, severe jackets, and long skirts were the height of career woman chic back in 1987. And, of course, Melanie Griffith made her mark on Wall Street as Tess McGill in *Working Girl* when she traded her big hair and spandex dresses for more closely cropped locks and a tailored suit.

A friend of mine who is a highly accomplished sales executive shared with me her reflections on dressing for the workplace during the early days of her career:

> When I was the only female on the trading floor at a bank, I was one of the top producers so I could "push the envelope a little" every once in a while. Sometimes I dressed like a man—I wore pin stripe pants with suspenders, slicked my hair back with grease, and wore exaggerated big black glasses. Some days I dressed like a schoolmarm—quite prissy and uptight—just to keep them all guessing and not let them figure me out. I basically used regular clothing as my "costume" for each day. Since I was the only female, all 14 traders constantly picked on me and tried to "break" me. It was all in good fun, and not exactly mean, but I threw curve balls back at them and they didn't know what to do.

Women have asserted themselves in the workplace enough that dressing exactly like a man is no longer necessary for success. Nor do you need to feel obliged to push the envelope by costuming yourself, as my friend once did. Rather, you can stay true to yourself by wearing feminine clothes, if that's what makes you comfortable.

On the other hand, some women have the wrong notion when it comes to femininity. Does "dressing like a girl" mean that you should emphasize your sexuality to get ahead? Absolutely not. If you've seen the television show *30 Rock,* you know that Liz Lemon's (Tina Fey) assistant Cerie loves to wear inappropriate clothing to the office. During one episode, Liz has to convince Cerie to wear a bra to work—if she wants to be taken seriously. Cerie's response? "Oh, I don't actually want to work in television. Career-wise, I'm just going to marry rich and then design handbags." Although the situation is played for comic effect, the message is clear: women who dress inappropriately won't get ahead in any real career.

SKIRT TIP

Dressing too much like a man in the workplace can come off as gimmicky. Strive for a polished work wardrobe that still reflects your femininity.

Many men—and some women, for that matter—will tell you that sex sells. Although that is true, especially since it is a multi-billion dollar industry, it is not necessarily true in the professional arena. There is a definite dividing line between what's appropriate for work and what's appropriate for a nightclub.

Case in Point: Sex Doesn't Necessarily Sell— Modesty Does

In the early 1990s, I was working a trade show with several other sales associates. Some of the men in the office told the women that were working the show that they should wear short skirts and low-cut blouses. The men, of course, would be wearing suits. "Why should I wear short skirts and low-cut blouses?" I asked. Their response was, "Sex sells. You get them in the booth and we'll close them." Although I held my tongue and we did *not* dress to their liking, I did conduct an informal survey with all the men that visited our booth. I asked them three questions:

Do you prefer women that are going to sell you a serious product to be wearing professional attire or evening attire? The majority said professional attire.

Which woman would you take more seriously in an office? Most everyone said the professional attire.

If you were going out for the evening, which would you prefer? It was almost a unanimous vote for evening attire. (I just wanted to make sure they were honest and breathing!)

Now let's move to a different trade show. This was a construction show and the women arrived professionally dressed. We were the only exhibitors that had nothing to do with construction, so that alone set us apart. The first night the trade show opened, I was working our booth with one other woman. We overheard two men saying, "Isn't she beautiful? She really is gorgeous." Needless to say we were flattered and excited that we heard that even *without* wearing short skirts. However, as the two men got a little closer, we found out that those wonderful remarks were aimed at a beautiful truck that was parked next to us! In this case, dressing professionally was neither an asset nor a liability.

In both of these examples, sex didn't sell in the professional arena. To further emphasize this point, here are some interesting statistics from a survey conducted by *Work Your Image*:

- 75 percent of Americans say that a woman's appearance on the job is likely to affect whether she is taken seriously.

- 64 percent of respondents believe that a woman's appearance on the job affects whether she will be considered for a raise or promotion.

- 84 percent of Americans say that a woman's appearance on the job is likely to affect whether she is asked to represent her company at outside meetings.

- 66 percent of respondents believe that a woman's appearance on the job is likely to affect whether she is given new challenges, responsibilities and opportunities.

USA Today reporter Maria Puente summed it up the best in her article "How NOT to Dress for Work," in which she wrote, "Of course, no one wants to return to the silly old days when women could be chastised—or even banned from the U.S. Senate floor—for wearing a pantsuit. But many people say the pendulum has swung too far." Don't let the pendulum swing too far when it comes to your professional attire!

Appropriate Wardrobe Options for Women

Our male counterparts don't have as difficult a job as we do to dress professionally. Is it a suit, a jacket and pants, or a shirt and pants? They can dress up with a tie or dress down by taking the tie off. In the winter, they can add a sweater or vest and in the summer they can wear a short-sleeved shirt. In fact, if you look up dressing professionally for men, you will see longer and shorter versions of these descriptions above, but not too many additions or deletions. Really nothing has changed much for men since the 1950s—except perhaps a recommendation to cover up tattoos and remove any facial piercings—and there are not many suggestions for men to dress professionally. Women's professional attire, however, is an entirely different story.

The guidelines for appropriate women's attire have changed drastically over the past several decades. There is no final say about what we should or shouldn't wear, what is or is not appropriate, and what the alternatives are. Personally, I recommend the following guidelines for women, which came from an article in *USA Today* in 2004.

<u>Probably OK</u>

Sleeveless tops
Leather mules
Multiple gold earrings
Highlights
Above-the-knee skirts
Cropped pants in dressy fabrics
Lace camisole peeking from blouse

<u>Not OK</u>

Spaghetti straps
Rubber flip-flops
Nose rings
Blue hair or other colors not found in nature
Micro-minis
Shorts
Underwear as outerwear

With these guidelines in mind, let's go over some of the choices in clothing that we have:

Suits: Many industries have dress codes, and for some that includes suits. They can be pantsuits (which some say are not feminine enough) as well as skirt suits.

Pants: If you do wear pants, make sure they aren't too tight and that you have no visible panty lines. (Fortunately, there are new remedies for that problem.) Make sure the pants are not cut too low so that if you bend down, you inadvertently remind someone of their local plumber.

Skirts: The length of your skirt is important. Regardless of the latest fashion trends, skirts should always be knee length or longer, and you should stay away from slits and tight skirts. To find the right fit, try the skirt on in front of a mirror. Do everything you would do in the office in front of the mirror—sit down and cross your legs, reach for something, stoop down. If you see too much leg (or, heaven forbid, your panties), the skirt is too short.

Tops: You can wear a spaghetti strap top if you plan

on keeping your jacket on all day. If not, wear a top that is not as revealing. In either case, make sure you are not showing too much cleavage—and be mindful of whether others can see down your top when you bend forward!

Shoes: Choose shoes that are comfortable and appropriate for the office—and save your *super-high* high-heels for your evenings out.

Pantyhose/tights: The rule of thumb is that whenever any part of your leg is showing, you should be wearing pantyhose, thigh-high stockings, or tights.

Case in Point: Smart Women Wear Hose

I am often criticized for wearing pantyhose in 100-degree weather. But if I am going into the office, conducting a training session, or speaking on stage and I'm wearing a skirt or dress, my outfit is not complete without some kind of hose. Yes, I get the eye-rolling...and it comes from men as well as women. All I can say is that it's better to be overdressed than leave a bad impression.

One time I was leading a very large training class, and when I was not on stage I was sitting at a table with both men and women. Another trainer was on stage with a short skirt and bare legs. The comments were *not* complimentary—and those were from the men. Their biggest gripe was that she was not wearing pantyhose. I rest my case.

If you have any question at all about what you are planning to wear, the outfit probably isn't appropriate.

In her book *Play Like a Man, Win Like a Woman*, Gail Evans states that your clothes should demonstrate that you are dressed appropriately for the playing field of your career—you are wearing the right uniform to look like part of the team and achieve your goals. At the same time, you want to feel confident about your wardrobe, which should reflect your creativity and personal style. Clothing announces to the world not just who you are, notes Evans, but the professional that you aspire to become.

It's a fact of life that men and women have different physiological and cultural foundations. The corporate world does not need a new crop of competitive, masculine women. Rather, women can develop a successful career in sales by recognizing the differences between the genders, adapting their communication style to their audience, operating within their relational strengths, and maintaining a professional demeanor at all times. Similarly, businesses can thrive in today's market environment when they let men be men and women be women, celebrating the differences and empowering associates to work within their core giftings. In the next chapter, we'll look at effective strategies that sales managers can use to recruit and retain talented female sales professionals.

SKIRT WISDOM

- Women should use their natural tendency to network and build relationships when looking for a job.

- Understanding that women are relational and men are transactional can prepare you for the interview process.

- Women commonly have to prove themselves in sales while men are assumed capable.

- Adapting to both male and female communication styles can alleviate tension in the workplace.

- Extreme behaviors, like being overly aggressive or overly emotional, can hurt your career.

- Appearances matter—women should take extra care to dress professionally.

CHAPTER EIGHT

RECRUITING, RETAINING AND PROMOTING WOMEN IN SALES

We've spent a lot of time talking about the importance of female-centric training in the workforce. But this kind of training only really works if you have women working in your organization to begin with. A lot has changed since the 1960s, when most women didn't work outside the home at all. Fast forward about 50 years—women have joined almost every industry you can think of, from aerospace engineering to zoology. But this doesn't mean that women are represented in proportionate numbers, or that their pay is equal to that of their male colleagues.

Let me throw some statistics at you. For the first time, women now account for half (49.9 percent) of the U.S. workforce. But guess what? Women account for nearly 59 percent of U.S. workers making less than $8 per hour, according to a recent report in *College Times*. In addition, women earn only 77 cents for every dollar a man earns. The statistics are worse for minority women: African-American women earn only 64 cents for every dollar a man earns, and Hispanic women only earn 52 cents for every dollar. What's more, only 4 out of every 10 businesses worldwide can boast women in senior level management. We may have come a long way, baby—but we still have a long way to go.

We've already talked about the influence women wield over major purchases in the marketplace. Obviously, a savvy sales associate will use the techniques presented here to engage female clientele and harness the benefit of that purchasing power. Having higher numbers of women in your workforce likewise can work to your company's advantage. A Pew Research Center Social and Demographic Trends survey on leadership found that Americans believe that women in the workforce are more honest, compassionate, and creative than men. This doesn't mean that men cannot also be honest, compassionate, and creative. It just means that this is the overarching perception by those people who will be your clients.

SKIRT TIP
Understandably, women buyers often gravitate toward female sales associates, because they 'speak the same language.' Increasing the number of women on your sales team can have a powerful impact on your bottom line

A study by Catalyst called, "The Bottom Line: Connecting Corporate Performance and Gender Diversity," found that companies with the highest representation of women on their senior management teams had:

- 35 percent higher return on equity

- 34 percent higher total return to shareholders

- 42 percent higher return on sales

Those cold hard facts send the clear message that women contribute to successful corporate bottom lines. Add those figures to public perception of women in the workforce and you have two very compelling reasons to make women an integral part of your team. But this means you need to recruit, retain, and promote them in ways that speak to their own unique needs. To do so, you must find ways to communicate with female employees, to create and define the ideal workplace, and to motivate them so they stick around.

Recruitment: Getting Those High Heels in the Door
The first step of the hiring process is recruitment. With 49.9 percent of the U.S. workforce being women, failing to recruit female associates will cut your options in half. If you are involved in recruitment for your organization, how can you position your company so that it offers a lot of appeal for women seeking employment? Three key factors—communication, workplace, and motivation—can be combined to make your company more attractive to women.

Remember the differences between the ways men and women communicate. Men want to get straight to the facts and close the deal. They then look to develop a working relationship. On the other hand, women want to build a relationship with a company and often perceive the interview process as that crucial first step toward becoming a member of the corporate family. A female candidate will ask a lot of probing questions, and the entire session is relationship-driven. Men, on the other hand, will want to "sell" the company, focusing mainly on salary and benefit options. At the end of the interview, the male recruiter thinks he has made a successful sale, while the female candidate thinks the two of you have taken your first step on the path of your future together.

To attract more women to your company, consider changing tactics for female candidates versus male candidates. When interviewing female applicants, focus on how your company can build a lasting relationship and encourage those relational metaphors.

SKIRT TIP
Define and tell your organization's story as part of your recruiting efforts. Help female recruits understand your company culture, so they can feel the sense of connection they naturally desire.

How can you entice a woman to form a relationship with your company? Think of it this way: men are more utilitarian than women. For example, a man may be more interested in the engine size of the car he's purchasing; women may be more concerned with the cup holders and heated seats. Men may appreciate style but are swayed

by the functional aspects of a purchase, while women
may value functional components but opt for the most
practical features. When it comes to recruitment, men
are more likely to make a decision based solely on
salary and potential bonuses, but women want to find the
ideal workplace—a place to call home—not just a big
paycheck. A big paycheck is always nice, but women are
more motivated by factors related to their lifestyle and
long-term goals, such as:

- Flexible hours and on-site childcare

- Network groups

- Leadership and development programs specifically
  geared toward women

- A company that distinguishes between and
  celebrates both men and women

- An environment that teaches women how to make
  the most of their inborn traits

- Mentoring programs

By providing a workplace that offers plenty of
relational benefits and detailing those benefits to your
recruits, you are more likely to attract female candidates
who will be invested in your company for the long term.

Although it may be awkward at first, women can
and should be integrated into more traditionally-male
occupations. Any awkwardness can be passed over if
women and men simply work together to create a more
accepting work environment, one that balances the

boys' club way of doing business with a female-centric perspective.

Part of this balance goes back to recognizing women's tendency to operate from an experiential rather than transactional perspective. Remember how women think when they shop, taking in the sights, sounds and smells of their environment in addition to the checklist of considerations that weigh into their purchasing decision? Those same considerations affect our level of comfort and productivity in the workplace. Now, we do not need drapes on the windows and fresh flowers on every desk, but we also don't want to be lost in a sea of cold gray cubicles. Creating an attractive environment will make female associates feel valued, and likely will go largely unnoticed by their male colleagues so long as the space is clean and professional, not girly.

SKIRT TIP Women have a natural tendency to "nest" and create a livable environment for themselves at work as well as at home. Comfortable and stylish office furniture, a few plants, or artwork on the walls can make your office more appealing to female recruits.

Similarly, in the same way that women buyers want to foster a relationship with a sales associate to feel confident in their decision, female sales professionals want to have a strong relationship with their employer and co-workers to feel secure. By building a workplace that fosters relationships, you can provide the feeling of security and connection that women desire. No longer will men feel like women are "crashing the party" if they join the ranks of the good old boys' club. Instead, women will feel welcome, a crucial part of the team, and they'll stick around with your company, boosting your bottom line well into the future.

A final note on this issue: As your company adapts its recruiting strategies to attract more women into the ranks, when it comes to hiring decisions, the final selection process should be no different than it is for male candidates. Women should be judged on their qualifications, achievements or references in exactly the same way men are. However, when recruiting female candidates, the way you, as a manager, communicate your company's benefits, the office environment you create and the motivational tools you offer must be presented in a way that your female sales force finds attractive.

Retention: Making the Most of Your Investment

Without a doubt, the most costly aspect of the employment process is recruiting and training qualified associates. Once you get skilled female employees in the door, what can you do to make the most of your investment? How can you get them to keep coming in, day after day?

Every good sales manager knows that to motivate your employees, you need to offer incentives. By motivating employees, you will engage them emotionally, not only winning their loyalty but also helping them push past perceived boundaries to achieve shared goals. This is how you separate the wheat from the chaff; a highly motivated employee will be much more likely to rise through the ranks than one who could care less. But be aware that there are key gender differences when it comes to motivating your staff. Cigars, golf, NASCAR, and strip bars are probably not the best prize choices for your female salespeople.

SKIRT TIP

When it comes to perks, apply the same thinking as you would when buying a birthday gift. Look for something that appeals to the recipient, not your own tastes or long-standing tradition.

Everyone is motivated differently; yet, the one thing that most sales managers don't do a good job of is talking with each team member about what motivates them. If, as a leader, you inspire your team members to reach specific goals, knowing they will appreciate the reward on a personal level, you very well could see success rates skyrocket. As a manager, you've got the power to discover what emotionally engages your sales professionals and offer incentives that speak to their personal preferences. This works for both men and women.

What's the secret? The same approach that works for clients works for employees; it's about building relationships and asking questions. Connect with your team members. Ask them what motivates them most in their lives—either in their professional careers, or even their personal lives. By motivating your star players, you give them the incentives they need to do a good job for you—and to continue doing that job so well that they rise through the ranks of your organization in no time at all.

Case in Point: NASCAR vs. Pink Cadillacs

Once I worked for a large insurance company that recognized individuals' successes with rounds of golf, new golf clubs, or tickets to see the local professional baseball team. Do you think that motivated all of us?

Being competitive, I always won any contest thrown my way. I went to the Masters and NASCAR. I even won a fishing pole and a tackle box. I would have preferred something that was of more interest to me—but no one asked. A spa treatment, a gift certificate to Nordstrom, jewelry or something equally feminine would have gone a long way and would have been something to push me to reach an even higher level.

Mary Kay Ash, the founder of Mary Kay Cosmetics, was a genius when it came to motivating her (mostly female) employees. Frustrated when a man she trained was promoted over her head at work, Ash quit her job at Stanley Home Products. She began to write a book about the ideal business for women, but that book segued into the original business plan for Mary Kay Cosmetics. The infamous pink Cadillacs—first awarded in 1969—were only a part of Ash's motivational reward program for employees. She developed a system that catered to her female workers, offering world-class travel and diamond jewelry. The results speak for themselves. Ash started the company in 1963 with a $5000 investment. By 2008, the company boasted 1.7 million consultants worldwide and wholesale sales in excess of $2.2 billion. How? She not only catered to the tastes of female customers, but also to the preferences of the women who made up her sales force.

Harness the power of incentives and just watch your business thrive. For women, this goes beyond giving them two tickets to the game or a gold necklace and slapping them on the back. To show women you appreciate their work, you must make them feel that they are a part of the team with a long-term strategy for success. Here are a few strategies to accomplish this feat:

- Provide equal opportunity for men and women

- Respect each other's skill sets and knowledge

- Be mindful of a woman's need for relationships

- Motivate women specifically to their needs and preferences, not those of their male counterparts.

Finally, sales executives should look for opportunities to promote their female associates to the masses. For example, a company might post an article on its website about a saleswoman who received a promotion or won an award in recognition of her work, or encourage her to submit a commentary to a well-known trade publication. These types of public affirmations will go a long way toward making female associates feel they are respected and valued members of the sales force, and will also attract other talented women to your company.

Promotion: Providing a Pathway to Professional Growth

Is there an actual economic benefit for companies that promote female employees? After all, we now know the statistics about women in the workforce, and how beneficial a diverse employee base can be for a company. But what about allowing women to break through glass ceilings? What impact can that have on a company?

A Pepperdine University study published in the *Harvard Business Review* makes a powerful case for encouraging women to rise in the ranks. The 2001 study analyzed data from more than 200 Fortune 500 companies concerning the gender makeup of their senior management and board members from 1980-1998. The findings showed that the 25 best firms for women outperformed the industry medians on three measures:

- Calculated as a percent of revenue, their profits were 34 percent higher.

- Calculated as a percent of assets, profits were 18 percent higher.

- Calculated as a percent of stockholders' equity, profits were 69 percent higher.

Promoting women likely will be a boon to your business—so what is the best plan for putting theory into practice?

Earlier, I mentioned that mentorship programs were a powerful benefit, one that gets more women interested in your company. I feel very strongly that companies need mentoring programs for women that provide focused development and increased exposure. Research indicates that a mentored employee is likely to form a strong bond with you and your company, becoming someone you can count on in tough times.

With a mentoring program, the protégé benefits by having the opportunity to learn faster, to observe and emulate role models, and to demonstrate skills. These factors can only increase her self-confidence. In addition, protégés have an opportunity to dry run critical decisions to a confidential, nonjudgmental sounding board. But the benefits don't go just one way. Mentors have a broadened sense of responsibility, a sense of being trusted by the organization, and the challenge of advising rather than directing. Mentors also learn from their protégés and enjoy the satisfaction of seeing someone grow. For many sales leaders and managers, it can be a way of paying back a past mentor of their own.

SKIRT TIP

Assigning a mentor to a female associate can make her feel that she has someone championing her career growth and strengthen her loyalty to your organization.

Make mentoring part of the job description for new managers, and develop a structured mentoring program with clearly defined goals and measurable deliverables. Not only will such a program help those women coming through the ranks, it will pave the way for future recruits. Mentoring relationships give everyone—men and women—another reason to stay and grow with your company, which reduces personnel costs. Mentoring is the best way to reduce costly turnover, because you develop your star employees and increase both their productivity and job satisfaction.

Another way to guarantee promotion of female workers is through tuition reimbursement and executive coaching programs. Each year, *Working Mother* magazine publishes lists of the best companies in America for women. These lists provide a glimpse of the companies that offer the best in benefits for female employees, including traditionally female-friendly pluses, like paid child care, paid maternity leave, and flex time. The magazine also publishes a second list each year, detailing which companies provide the most fertile ground for professional growth for women. What's the crucial difference between the two lists? Without a doubt, the companies that offer tuition reimbursement or coaching programs to their employees see a much greater rise in female employees through the upper echelons.

Tuition reimbursement also retains more employees, reducing the amount of turnover a company sees. According to a case study conducted by Colleen Flaherty for the National Bureau of Economic Research, companies that implemented tuition reimbursement programs saw a significant decrease in employee turnover. This is reinforced by an article in the *Baltimore Business Journal,* titled "More companies are offering tuition reimbursement for workers," from late 2007. According to the article, more small businesses are jumping on the tuition reimbursement bandwagon to stay competitive and are seeing more employees stick around—even after receiving an advanced education at the company's expense. What does this mean for your business? Every chance you give women to further their education is a chance for your company to grow.

In the end, the strategies for recruiting, retaining and promoting women are very similar to the strategies employed with men—they just speak to female-centric values and communication style. Men look for features and benefits; women look for a long-term relationship. Men enjoy incentives that involve athletics and competition; women prefer perks that make them look better and feel better. Men value prestige; women value flexibility. If you understand and address these dynamics, you can build and grow a powerful sales force that embraces and empowers associates of either gender.

SKIRT WISDOM

- Recruiting, retaining, and promoting women in your company can work wonders for your bottom line.

- While men are more concerned about salary, women often will accept a job based on benefits, such as flex time, child care, and leadership programs.

- When motivating women to succeed, provide rewards that really inspire them.

- Women in the workplace want to be treated equally, not identically.

- Engage your team by asking them what motivates them most in life.

- Implementing a mentorship program can help you retain and promote good employees.

SELLING IN A SKIRT

CONCLUSION

When I first started my career, men took their secretaries to lingerie shows at lunch and drank martinis on the job. Few women had professional career aspirations, and those that worked in a business environment were often viewed as arm candy or limited to administrative roles. Women who spoke up, spoke out, and climbed the corporate ladder were viewed as revolutionaries. A friend of mine, also named Judy, who is an accomplished sales executive shared a story recently about how she caused shockwaves, when—as the only female on the trading floor at a bank—she wore a leopard print skirt. She could hear the guys on the floor whispering on the squawk box to traders around the country: "Judy wore a leopard skirt!" This simple wardrobe choice—so common in any modern woman's wardrobe—was a big deal back then.

"They couldn't fire me. I was the top producer," she said, as she recalled the early days of her career. "When you are at the top of your game, it's hard to get fired and you can call the shots within certain boundaries."

I share her story with you because as I finish writing this book, I am reminded again of how much things have changed. When I first started out, women were encouraged not to make waves. Now, women are free to choose any career they wish. And they have. As women infiltrate formerly male-centric industries, they may find that their natural ways of communicating and establishing relationships are counterintuitive to the ways that men think. This can either cause a lot of friction or an opportunity for growth, depending on how you choose to view it.

Men and women are inherently dissimilar. The disparities start with the fact that our brains are actually wired differently. Our culture also treats us differently. But rather than dissect the "whys" of physiology or sociology behind this diversity, professionals in the workforce need to embrace it to survive. For as we all know, the new driving force behind sales is no longer the traditional transactional model. The consultative approach, once thought to be exclusively feminine, is overtaking almost every industry—and it is especially relevant in sales.

Companies that stubbornly insist on utilizing a strictly transactional technique for sales run the risk of missing the crucial opportunity to connect with female buyers. As social media continues to integrate relational tactics into our society, the consultative approach drives the biggest sales. Since women are naturally gifted at this type of sales technique, smart companies will recruit, retain, and promote women to their upper echelons. The company that wants to survive in today's competitive marketplace will also cease training methods that force a "cookie-cutter" mentality onto all sales professionals.

Implementing the strategies in this book will help you embrace this new dynamic so that you can accomplish three major goals: increase your sales, gather referrals, and establish productive, long-term relationships with your clients. By doing so you not only increase your bottom line and grow your business exponentially, but you can also kiss your days of cold calling goodbye.

This doesn't mean that companies have to switch to two types of training: one for men and one for women. Nor does it mean that women should adapt to the traditional male-centric sales model to survive. What it does mean is that we should customize our approaches—whether we are working on training new recruits, retaining a top-drawer team, or starting out on the sales force as a fresh-faced newbie. Take what works best for the given situation, borrowing strategies from both the traditional, more male way of doing things as well as the more relational, female way of doing things. The most important thing to remember is to adapt your approach for the given situation.

Have you ever seen the movie *My Fair Lady*? In the film, Professor Henry Higgins poses the famous question:

> *Why can't a woman be more like a man?*
>
> *Men are so honest, so thoroughly square.*
>
> *Eternally noble, historically fair.*
>
> *Who, when you win, will give your back a pat.*
>
> *Why can't a woman be like that?*

Aside from the fact that they two genders have different physiological and cultural foundations, I hope we can now agree that the world does not need a new crop of competitive, masculine women.

With apologies to Professor Higgins, I pose this question instead, "Why can't a man be more like a woman?"

Perhaps the best question of all is, "Why can't men be men, and women be women, and we'll celebrate our differences?"

I hope this book encourages you to celebrate the differences between the genders, and to look beyond business as usual to find a truly personalized approach to sales—one that will help you achieve lasting success. Now go out and make some waves!

GET CONNECTED

For more information on Judy Hoberman, to schedule her to speak at your next event, or to have Judy develop a sales training program for your organization, please contact her through any of these media:

Website	www.sellinginaskirt.com
Facebook	facebook.com/sellinginaskirt
Twitter	@sellinginaskirt
Linkedin	http://linkd.in/judyh
Email	judy@sellinginaskirt.com